WHO SAID THAT?

The Stories Behind Familiar Expressions

**For Readers, Writers, Word Lovers, and Trivia Buffs,
Fresh Ink Group Explains Whence Come
Those Phrases That Color Everyday Speech**

WHO SAID THAT?

The Stories Behind Familiar Expressions

For Readers, Writers, Word Lovers, and Trivia Buffs,
Fresh Ink Group Explains Whence Come
Those Phrases That Color Everyday Speech

J. Ajlouny

Fresh Ink Group
Guntersville

WHO SAID THAT?
The Stories Behind Familiar Expressions

For Readers, Writers, Word Lovers, and Trivia Buffs, Fresh Ink Group Explains Whence Come Those Phrases That Color Everyday Speech

Fresh Ink Group
An Imprint of:
The Fresh Ink Group, LLC
Box 931
Guntersville, AL 35976
Email: info@FreshInkGroup.com
FreshInkGroup.com

Edition 1.0	1997
Edition 2.0	2016
Edition 2.1	2017

Book design by Ann E. Stewart

Cover design by Stephen Geez

BISAC Subject Headings:
REF019000 REFERENCE / Quotations
LAN014000 LANGUAGE ARTS & DISCIPLINES / Reference
REF022000 REFERENCE / Thesauri

Library of Congress Control Number: 2016949885

ISBN: 978-1-936442-31-7 Paper-cover
ISBN: 978-1-396442-32-4 Hard Cover
ISBN: 978-1-936442-70-6 eBook Editions

To admirers of literature everywhere

Contents

Introduction

Chapter 1. Who Said That? 1
Quotations for which the source is not widely known

Chapter 2. Who Really Said It? 27
Quotations often erroneously attributed

Chapter 3. What Was Actually Said? 47
Quotations often misquoted

Chapter 4. What Was Really Meant? 59
Quotations often misunderstood

Chapter 5. Why Was It Said? 69
Quotations in their original context

Chapter 6. Who Repeated That? 91
Recycled quotations in new contexts

About the Author 99

Alphabetical Index i

Introduction

John Bartlett (1820–1905) rendered a great service to the English-speaking world when his *Familiar Quotations* was first published in Boston in 1855. So mixed was the reaction that he was compelled to revise, supplement, and re-edit it three times before his next major work, a concordance of the works of Shakespeare, was published in 1894. During those intervening years he and his work were the subject of much debate, some praise and a good deal of criticism. The major thrust of the critical remarks was that he included obscure quotes while neglecting the more popular expressions of the day.

Bartlett's reluctance to include colloquial expressions rested upon two points. First, he sought to distance his work from the hugely successful *Dictionary of Americanisms* (1848) collected by his namesake, John Russell Bartlett (1805–1886) of Rhode Island. Second, Bartlett sought to develop a useful work that satisfied his own penchant for inquiry into classical literature. He thus set about collecting a list of formal quotations that he thought should be familiar to the average educated American. His purpose was not to develop a reference work; rather, he sought to create a vast summary of recorded western thought, a book that readers could cuddle up with when the desire to commune with Archimedes or Zola struck them. But, as we shall see, "the best laid plans of mice and men often go astray."

Good quotes are popular, or should I say, popular quotes are good, because they are a nifty way to say something that frequently needs to be said. They are handy expressions that are useful in a wide variety of circumstances. Yet they have become so familiar to us that we fail to ponder their authors or the context in which they were first written or uttered. This collection of popular quotations and the circumstances of their seminal publication is a modest attempt to remedy this neglect.

Take for example, "You've hit the nail on the head." How many hundreds of times have you heard this expression? You know exactly what it means and it is difficult to imagine someone using it in error. It's that familiar. And just as you wouldn't think of asking your grandfather the name of his first girlfriend—not because it would be wrong but because you just never thought about it—you probably haven't given any thought to who originated this popular expression, where and why. But as it turns out, it's quite an interesting story.

Who Said That? is filled with the stories of how popular quotations were given birth. But be forewarned. In many cases these tales are subject to speculation. Just as no one can credibly claim to have originated a proverb, some quotations have such a checkered past that it is impossible to trace them with utter certainty. In many instances the explanations provided here may not be the only ones. As Bartlett intended his work be one of learning, I intend this work be one of fun while learning. If it stands for anything, I would hope it fosters a sense of curiosity in the reader to question what is read and what is heard. You never know, the nugget of a fascinating tale may be soon discovered.

This collection of stories and anecdotes about the origin of popular quotes owes its existence to my love of the writings of G. K. Chesterton (1874–1936), the prodigious British journalist, essayist, novelist, playwright, literary critic, philosopher, and lecturer extraordinaire. It was at a conference dedicated to his literary tradition that this book was conceived. Though Chesterton is regarded as the second most frequently quoted writer in the English language, sadly none of his remarkable quotations have won their way into the language to be called "popular." It's a shame because his wit and epigrams are unequaled, and paradoxical.

To John Peterson, Dale Ahlquist, Dan Krotz, Sister Bernadette Sheridan, and my fellow Chestertonians, I offer my thanks for their contrbutions, suggestions, and good cheer. To Marilyn Krol Zerlak, Tempest Moore, Berg Djelderian, Lawrence Ajlouny, Nezza Bendele, Tahira K. Ahmad, and my bookish old friend Hedger Breed, I offer my thanks for their efforts in assisting me with this task. To Stephen Geez and Ann Stewart at Fresh Ink Group, I offer my thanks for their indulgence, and to Gwen Foss I offer my special thanks for everything else. She deserves it!

Joseph S. Ajlouny
Detroit

CHAPTER 1
WHO SAID THAT?

Quotations for Which the Source Is Not Widely Known

"Leave no stone unturned."
Euripides (c.485–406 BCE)

Greek playwright Euripides is ranked with Aeschylus and Sophocles as the greatest of Greek dramatists. He prospered at the court of Archelaus, king of Macedonia, and it is said he won first prize in five dramatic contests. His tragedy Herakleidae contains the expression "turn every stone," which over time has metamorphosed into the common expression we hear today.

"Necessity is the mother of invention."
Plato (427–347 BCE)

The political discourse of Greek philosopher Plato is legendary. The famous statement appears in Book II of his masterpiece, *The Republic* (c.375 BCE). The sage's premise is that necessity is the creator of the ideal state, one which would administer justice, uphold the law and provide a stable society whose individuals could prosper to the best of their capabilities. The original quote translates as, "The true creator is necessity, who is the mother of our invention." The folk process has expanded upon Plato's wisdom to produce the common saying, "Necessity is the mother of invention and peril is the father."

"A friend in need is a friend indeed."
Titus Maccius Plautus (c.255–184 BCE)

Roman playwright Plautus' comedy *Epidicus* is the first known source of this ancient saying, which appears in the original as, "A friend in need is the finest thing a man can have." The irony is that the speaker, Periphanes, is in the process of being fooled by his own slave. Ordered to find him a girl, the slave, hoping to earn more money, brings in a young woman whom he claims is his daughter. Later, he sells her for another girl who turns out to be Periphanes' long-lost daughter. The only happy person in the end of the play is the hapless Periphanes, who remains blissfully ignorant of the machinations of his devious slave.

"It makes no sense to flog a dead horse."
Titus Maccius Plautus (c.255–184 BCE)

Although its literal meaning belabors the obvious, its figurative meaning clearly suggests that it is futile to carry on a fruitless endeavor. In seventeenth century England, "working out the dead horse" meant working off a debt you will never be able to pay. Plautus, whose play *Epidicus* contains the earliest known reference to this well worn saying, was a Roman writer of lively, bawdy comedies based on Greek originals. Many of his characters and stories were recycled in the twentieth century in a popular musical play entitled A Funny Thing Happened on the Way to the Forum.

"Love conquers all."
Virgil (70–19 BCE)

Roman poet Publius Vergilius Maro, better known as Virgil, wrote the pastoral poem *Eclogues* from 40–37 BCE. In this lengthy opus, Virgil writes of the power and tyranny of the god of love. The protagonist Gallus, forlorn because his love has left him and he no longer finds joy in life, succumbs to this simple truth: "No toil of ours can change that god... Love conquers all; let us, too, yield to Love!"

"Bad news travels fast."
Plutarch (c.45–c.125)

Greek biographer Plutarch, an expert on ethics, wrote more than sixty essays on varying topics between the years 90–110, which were published under the title *Moralia*. In the chapter on courtesy, Plutarch attempts to redirect the energies of gossips, stating those who expend their curiosity learning about other people's lives should instead spend it learning about the world. His eloquently stated truth translates as,

How much more readily than glad events
Is mischance carried to the ears of men!

"A sound mind in a sound body."
Juvenal (c.60–c.140)

Little is known about the life of the Roman poet Juvenal (Decimus Junius Juvenalis), but his sixteen surviving bitter and biting Satires were admired and imitated by the likes of Samuel Johnson, Jonathan Swift, Alexander Pope and John Donne. In Satire 10, the poet writes that the best thing to pray for is Mens sana in corpore sano, "A healthy mind in a healthy body," because anything else one might want—power, wealth, beauty—can only cause trouble. In the same work, Juvenal prophetically declares the only things the public wants are "bread and circuses."

"Every man for himself."
Geoffrey Chaucer (c.1343–1400)

English poet Geoffrey Chaucer's classic, The Canterbury Tales (c.1387–1392), contains a series of stories related by pilgrims on their journey to Canterbury. The opus includes the story of a pair of cousins serving life terms in prison. The two men see a woman out their cell window and, as fate would have it, both fall in love with her. One cousin mentions the old story of two dogs fighting over a bone, and comments how each dog has to look out for its own interests. The character sums up the situation saying, "Ech man for hymself."

"Beggars can't be choosers."
John Heywood (1497–1580)

The Proverbs of John Heywood (1546) consists of an epic, proverb-laden poem. Many of the popular sayings we know today first appeared in print in this monumental work. In Part I, chapter 10, Heywood attempts to dispel the habit of marrying at too young an age. He writes of a young wife whose family scolds her for deciding to marry. Eager to repent, the woman does not ask her angry aunt what her punishment is to be, for she knows she is in no position to be demanding.

Nay, (quoth I), be they winners or losers,
Folk say always beggars should be no choosers.

"You can lead a horse to water but you can't make him drink."
John Heywood (1497–1580)

The Proverbs of John Heywood (1546) contains many of the apothegms and colloquialisms we know today. This expression is no exception. To demonstrate the wisdom of the familiar phrase, Heywood relates the story of a man whose uncle disapproves of his hedonistic lifestyle. The uncle reminds him that if he runs after pleasure, pleasure will run away; if he runs from pleasure, pleasure will chase him on. The advice, as written in the original, reads,

A man may well bring a horse to the water,
but he cannot make him drink without he will.

"Forewarned is forearmed."
Miguel de Cervantes (1547–1616)

Arguably the most famous of Spanish writers, Miguel de Cervantes is the celebrated author of *El Ingenioso Hidalgo Don Quixote de la Mancha*, better known to musical theater aficionados as *The Man of La Mancha* and to dazed high school students everywhere as Don Quixote. Considered his masterpiece, it was published in two parts in 1605 and 1615. The full quote, from Part I, Book I, chapter 17, reads, "Forewarned is forearmed; to be prepared is half the victory." Cervantes, a career soldier, became a writer after being wounded in the Battle of Lepanto, a naval engagement between the Ottoman Turks and the European allies, Spain and Venice, in 1571. Variations of dozens of other proverbial nuggets appear in Don Quixote.

"A man's home is his castle."
Sir Edward Coke (1552–1634)

A British jurist and member of parliament with a checkered career, Sir Edward Coke was described as being implacable but fair to the core. He is best known for his heroic resistance to the encroachments of the church and crown during the reign of queen Elizabeth I. The memorable phrase appears in the third volume of his legal treatise, *Institutes of British Law*. The full quote, translated from Latin, is, "For a man's house is his castle; for where shall a man be safe if it be not in his house?" The legal principle he established is that if a thief, while robbing a home, is killed by the master of the house, the killing is justified. Coke's habit of repeating this catch phrase in parliament was mimicked by revolutionaries of a dozen shades throughout Europe and the Americas.

"The devil can cite scripture for his purpose."
William Shakespeare (1564–1616)

The Merchant of Venice (1600) is among the many Shakespeare comedies with more quotable quotes than we know what to do with. In Act I, scene iii, a merchant named Antonio wants to borrow money, but the man who might give Antonio the money does not trust him to pay back the debt. Antonio delivers the well-known phrase to remind the creditor that what is on the outside is not always what lurks beneath. This proverb may already have been well known in Shakespeare's day, but his play is the earliest printed source.

"I have it here in black and white."
Ben Jonson (1572–1637)

Second only to William Shakespeare among British playwrights, Ben Jonson's plays are marked by sprightly dialogue, strong characterization and elaborate plotting. His first play, *Every Man in His Humour*, in which the quote appears in Act V, scene ii, was first performed in 1598, with William Shakespeare as a member of the cast. The phrase refers to a warrant.

"Do as I say, not as I do."
John Selden (1584–1654)

In Table Talk (1689), English scholar John Selden makes this all-too-common statement to enhance the similarly popular expression, "Practice what you preach." Table Talk is a recorded conversation, and to illustrate the principle, Selden gives the following example: "Preachers say, 'Do as I say, not as I do.' But if a physician had the same disease upon him that I have, and he should bid me do one thing and he do quite another, could I believe him?"

"Where there's a will, there's a way."
George Herbert (1593–1633)

English poet and rector George Herbert's posthumous work, Jacula *Prudentum* (1640), is the first published instance of this well-worn phrase. It appears as, "To him that will, ways are not wanting." As is the case with all proverbial sayings, this nugget of wisdom has been re-worded and repeated in many different forms. The first known instance of this saying in its present form occurs in *The Cruise of the Midge* (1836) by Scottish novelist Michael Scott (1789–1835).

"It made his mouth water."
Samuel Butler (1612–1680)

After the Puritans lost power in England, Butler wrote *Hudibras* (1663), a three part poem making light of their defeat. In the story, Sir Hudibras comes upon a widow whose luxurious assets and wealth draw him to want her, though she will have no part of it. Going against his oath, he tries to woo her with his courage and words of temptation.

And that his valor and the honor
H'had newly gained, might work upon her,
These reasons made his mouth to water
With am'rous longings to be at her.

"Stone walls do not a prison make."
Richard Lovelace (1618–1658)

A wealthy English landowner, colonel Richard Lovelace wrote the famous song *To Althea, from Prison*, in 1642 while being held by the government on a charge of sedition. Lovelace's song glorifies love and freedom, saying that as long as a man holds true to his convictions, he is, in all senses of the word, free. The quote appears in stanza four.

Stone walls do not a prison make, nor iron bars a cage;
Minds innocent and quiet take that for an hermitage;
If I have freedom in my love, and in my soul am free;
Angels alone that soar above, enjoy such liberty.

"The plot thickens."
George Villiers, Duke of Buckingham (1628–1687)

George Villiers' play, *The Rehearsal* (1671), is a spoof of the dramas being performed in England at the time. Its farfetched plot concerns a playwright who produces a play about a prince who is brought up by a fisherman who is arrested for murder. During an erratic rehearsal of the play within the play, the playwright explains his plot in painstaking detail to two guileless observers, and as the plot thickens, the playwright delivers the famous line, much to their dismay.

"The end justifies the means."
Matthew Prior (1664–1721)

May virtue be sacrificed for the sake of expediency? This is a question which has perplexed humanity for more than a millennium and has been explored in works by Greek, Roman and Arab philosophers. The first modern use of the statement occurs in a verse by Matthew Prior, an obscure British diplomat who wrote light verse and epigrams during his travels. Prior's satirical poem, Hans Carvel (1700), tells the story of an elderly, impotent farmer married to a young beauty whom he cannot satisfy. Fearing he's about to lose her to the charms of a more virile man, Hans contemplates making a deal with the devil to save her.

What if to spells I had Resource?
'Tis but to hinder something Worse
The End must justifie the Means:
He only Sins who Ill intends:
Since therefore 'tis to combat Evil;
'Tis lawful to employ the Devil.

"Hope springs eternal."
Alexander Pope (1688–1744)

The great English poet Alexander Pope's *An Essay on Man* (1733–1734) acknowledges the chain of being—that while there are creatures lower than Man, there are creatures higher as well. Pope reminds us that while we anxiously await the future, we should be hopeful in our ignorance and let things happen as they may.

Hope springs eternal in the human breast:
Man never is, but always to be, blest.
The soul, uneasy and confined from home,
Rests and expiates in a life to come.

"He was as sober as a judge."
Henry Fielding (1707–1754)

> English novelist and playwright Henry Fielding wrote *Don Quixote in England* (1734) as a burlesque of the classic tale. In his version, Quixote is caught up in a complicated love triangle: he loves Dorothea who loves Fairlove but whose father wants her to marry squire Badger. Finally Dorothea's father agrees to let her marry Fairlove, finding Badger boorishly drab. Badger is accused of being drunk, but retorts he is "as sober as a judge," leaving a sobering image in itself. Fielding was a lawyer and a justice of the peace before becoming a writer.

"A chip off the old block."
Edmund Burke (1729–1797)

> Quoted in *The Historical and the Posthumous Memoirs of Sir Nathaniel William Wraxall*, 1772–1784 (1815), member of parliament Edmund Burke's words were aimed squarely at William Pitt the Younger, 22-year-old first minister of George III. Pitt's father, the late prime minister William Pitt the Elder, was noted for his oratory skills which were said to rival those of Burke himself. Surprised by the youth's eloquence in opposition to a 1781 bill reforming the king's household budget, Burke exclaimed that Pitt "was not merely a chip off the old 'block,' but the old block itself."

"First in war, first in peace, and first in the hearts of his countrymen."
Henry Lee (1756–1818)

> It is generally known that this quote describes George Washington. What is not generally known is that the speaker was General Henry "Light-Horse Harry" Lee, and the occasion was George Washington's funeral in 1799. Lee was the father of another famous general, Robert E. Lee, who lamented after the bloody battle of Fredericksburg (1862), "It is well that war is so terrible. We should not grow too fond of it."

"It's not what it's cracked up to be."
Davy Crockett (1786–1836)

> As a frontiersman, Davy Crockett disapproved of the U.S. government's go-slow approach to westward expansion. He quickly became disenchanted with the supposed pro-annexation policies of president Martin Van Buren in 1838. Speaking of the president's reputation for machismo, Crockett opined, "It's not what it's cracked up to be," an assessment that persisted for decades. In the eighteenth century, the word crack in American vernacular meant "to boast."

"To the victor belongs the spoils."
William Learned Marcy (1786–1857)

President Andrew Jackson created the so-called "spoils system" in U.S. politics when, following his inauguration in 1829, he proposed to rid the government of corruption by firing two thousand federal administrators and appointing his supporters in their places. This policy did not, however, acquire a name until January 21, 1832, when New York senator William Marcy defended the practice in a debate with his famous exclamation. The description gained notoriety and was widely used, even after the Jacksonian policy on appointments was severely limited by the Civil Service Reform Act of 1883. Today, the president's authority to make appointments is commonly called the power of patronage.

"Mary had a little lamb."
Sarah Buell Hale (1788–1879)

A widow who took to writing to support her five children, Sarah Hale was a permanent fixture in Boston's social scene for fifty years. She was successful as the editor of her own women's magazine, Godey's Lady's Book. In 1830, she published *Poems for Our Children*, in which Mary's Lamb first appeared. The heroine and her charge might have languished in obscurity had a tune not been created for them soon after Hale's rhyme appeared in print. Mary's Lamb has since become the most widely known nursery song in American folklore. Sarah Hale is noteworthy for single-handedly convincing president Abraham Lincoln to reestablish Thanksgiving as a national holiday in the war-weary year of 1864. Her simple rhyme became the first words ever recorded, having been spoken by Thomas Edison during the testing of his sound phonograph in 1886.

"Absence makes the heart grow fonder."
Thomas H. Bayly (1797–1839)

Nathaniel Thomas Haynes Bayly was one of the most popular poets of the nineteenth century, but now he is quite forgotten. Before his poems passed into obscurity they went through a period of ridicule, as may be imagined by the title of his song, *Why Don't Men Propose, Mama?* Nevertheless, here is the final stanza of his Isle of Beauty, a place he is leaving with only memories to remind him of it.

When the waves are round me breaking,
As I pace the deck alone,
And my eye is vainly seeking
Some green leaf to rest upon;
When on that dear land I ponder,
Where my old companions dwell,
Absence makes the heart grow fonder —
Isle of Beauty, Fare thee well!

"It was a dark and stormy night."
Edward George Bulwer-Lytton (1803–1873)

An immensely prolific hack writer of Victorian novels, Edward George Bulwer-Lytton was once second in popularity to Charles Dickens. Today, however, he is best remembered as the inspiration for the Bulwer-Lytton Prize, awarded annually to the writer of the most overblown and comic-operatic opening sentence of an imaginary novel. However, Bulwer-Lytton didn't just write, "It was a dark and stormy night," and end there. That would certainly have shown too much mercy for his readers. The opening sentence, from Paul Clifford (1830), reads, in its entirety, "It was a dark and stormy night; the rain fell in torrents — except at occasional intervals, when it was checked by a violent gust of wind which swept up the streets (for it is in London that our scene lies), rattling along the housetops, and fiercely agitating the scanty flame of the lamps that struggled against the darkness." Cartoonist Charles Schulz, creator of *Peanuts*, often pictures Snoopy high atop his lonely, literary doghouse typing such a beginning.

"Remember the Alamo!"
Sidney Sherman (1805–1873)

Though he is regarded as the most inept military strategist in modern history, Mexico's eleven-time president and despot, Antonio Lopez de Santa Anna (c.1795–

1876), scored a decisive victory over Texas irregulars on March 6, 1836 at the San Antonio mission-turned-fortress called the Alamo. Despite being outnumbered forty to one, the ragtag Texans withstood the onslaught for 13 days. Left with no water or ammunition, the survivors allegedly offered to surrender. Their lives were not spared. In the end, all 202 defenders were killed, including frontier heroes Davy Crockett and Jim Bowie. The massacre so enraged the independence-minded Texans that they quickly accepted an offer of Federal assistance, and with the U.S. cavalry, won back the fort the following month. General Santa Anna was taken prisoner and forced to sign a treaty relinquishing Mexican claims to territory north of the Rio Grande. At the raising of the Texas flag, newly appointed commander Sidney Sherman eulogized the victims of the siege by urging the gathered to "remember the Alamo" as an example of valor for all times. Sherman's remark entered the popular vernacular, used most often as a symbolic phrase suggesting revenge is forthcoming.

"It seemed so near and yet so far away."
Alfred, Lord Tennyson (1809–1892)

It took ten years for English poet laureate Tennyson to write *In Memoriam* (1850), one of the great elegies of English literature. It was a poem of mourning, admiration and death. Tennyson wrote it about Arthur Henry Hallam, his close friend and future brother-in-law, while studying at college. Part of the poem is seen through the eyes of a husband and wife. Once intellectual equals, the husband's intelligence surpasses the wife's, but her love for him remains strong. In canto 97, Tennyson reflects that his relationship with Hallam was much the same.

He thrid the labyrinth of the mind,
He reads the secret of the star,
He seems so near and yet so far,
He looks so cold: She thinks him kind.

"Put your best foot forward."
Robert Browning (1812–1889)

In Respectability (1855), by English poet Robert Browning, two lovers comment on the customs of proper society and how their unconventional relationship merely lies on the outskirts. The man believes their love would not have developed as it did if they had been obligated to act within society's standards. They revel that their exclusion at least did not earn them time wasted.

I know! the world proscribes not love;
Allows my fingers to caress
Your lips' contour and downiness,
Provided it supply a glove.
The world's good word! the Institute!
Guizot receives Montalembert!
Eh? Down the court three lampions flare:
Put forward your best foot!

"They have a skeleton in their closet."
William Makepeace Thackeray (1811–1863)

A contemporary rival of Charles Dickens, British author William Thackeray began his career as an illustrator and satirist for the irreverent newsweekly *Punch*. He attained popular acclaim with his masterpiece *Vanity Fair* (1848). His other novels include *Henry Esmond* and its sequels, *The Virginians*, and *The Newcomes*, in which this quote appears in chapter 55. Thackeray mastered a luxurious style that held readers spellbound in nervous anticipation. With the turn of each page, a dark secret or disastrous flaw of character might bring wreck and ruin to his finely crafted protagonists.

"The public be damned."
William Henry Vanderbilt (1821–1885)

America's first railroad tycoon was a man of vision and flair. This quote, reportedly uttered during an 1870 meeting with his largest freight customers, was used by the press to ridicule him as unconcerned for the average man. Despite the fact that Vanderbilt both denied saying it and claimed the remark was taken out of context, the quote stuck to him and came to symbolize the single-minded greed of America's early millionaires, as well as the monopolist philosophy of the era. In reality, Vanderbilt was exceedingly philanthropic and supported a myriad of charitable causes.

"Now is the time for all good men to come to the aid of their party."
Charles E. Weller (1840–1925)

Scarcely anyone who learned to type before 1960 is not familiar with this "little finger exercise" created by New Jersey typewriter salesman Charles E. Weller. The phrase was composed to help learners become accustomed to the rigors of typewriting. It was used by millions of typing students until the newer, less political "The quick brown fox jumped over the lazy dog" was coined by an instructor whose name has been forever lost to posterity. There was an advantage to the new phrase, however; in using each letter of the alphabet at least once, it also served as a quick test to determine if the machine had any broken or missing keys.

"If a man bites a dog, that's news."
John B. Bogart (1845–1921)

As city editor of the New York Sun long before journalism was taught in college, John B. Bogart prided himself on his ability to determine newsworthy stories from bunk. His instructive declaration on what is and is not news was subsequently taught to cub reporters and is often repeated today. His full definition is as follows: "When a dog bites a man, that is not news because it happens all the time. But when a man bites a dog, that's news."

"Genius is one percent inspiration and ninety-nine percent perspiration."
Thomas Alva Edison (1847–1931)

American inventor Thomas Edison, not accustomed to tooting his own horn, gave this explanation for his success in an interview in 1916, shortly after taking a tour of Henry Ford's first automobile assembly line in Highland Park, Michigan. Hard work was a virtue both men espoused and practiced. In tribute to Edison, Ford founded the Edison Institute in Dearborn, Michigan, a sprawling indoor-outdoor museum complex dedicated to American innovation now known as the Henry Ford Museum and Greenfield Village. Edison's fully restored and equipped Menlo Park, New Jersey, laboratory is among the permanent highlights of the exhibition.

"Laugh and the world laughs with you; weep, and you weep alone."
Ella Wheeler Wilcox (1855–1919)

American poet and journalist Ella Wheeler Wilcox published the poem *Solicitude* in the New York Sun on February 25, 1883. Wilcox's emphasis on the darkness of loneliness was meant to contrast an age-old truth: despite moments of misery, people are always eager to share in joy. The complete quotation, found in the first stanza, reads, "Laugh and the world laughs with you;

weep, and you weep alone; for the sad old earth must borrow its mirth, but has trouble enough of its own."

"I can resist everything but temptation."
Oscar Wilde (1856–1900)

Irish-born Oscar Wilde, Victorian poet, playwright and novelist, is best remembered for his roguish and paradoxical wit. In his play, *Lady Windermere's Fan* (1891), Lord Darlington argues with the lady about her rigid code of morality. When Darlington tells her she is "fascinating," Lady Windermere reacts disapprovingly. "I couldn't help it," he explains. "I can resist everything but temptation." An examination of popular quotation collections reveals that many of the same or similar witticisms attributed to Oscar Wilde in Great Britain are attributed to Mark Twain in the United States.

"I don't believe in God because I don't believe in Mother Goose."
Clarence Darrow (1857–1938)

Celebrated attorney and labor activist Clarence Darrow is best known for heading the defense team of biology teacher John T. Scopes in the so-called "Monkey Trial" of 1925. Though Scopes was convicted of violating Tennessee's law against teaching ideas contrary to the Bible, Darrow regarded the trial as his finest hour. As a freethinker and Unitarian, he doubted the veracity of the biblical account of creation. He uttered the famous statement upon questioning from reporters after the guilty verdict was returned. Incidentally, Scopes' conviction was overturned two years later by the Tennessee Supreme Court in a decision which nonetheless upheld the law's constitutionality.

"It's better to die fighting than to live in slavery."
Emmeline Pankhurst (1858–1928)

Emmeline Pankhurst was a forceful political activist in the early decades of the twentieth century. An advocate of women's suffrage, she founded the Women's Social and Political Union in 1905. She and her daughters, Christabel, Sylvia and Adela, worked tirelessly to promote the ideal of equality for all. Appearing at the Army and Navy Hall in Petrograd, Russia (now St. Petersburg), in August 1917, she said, "Better that we should die fighting than be outraged and dishonored... Better to die than to live in slavery."

"The mighty Casey has struck out."
Ernest Laurence Thayer (1863–1940)

The all-American poem Casey at the Bat was first published in a San Francisco newspaper in 1888. Balladeer Thayer was said to have had an actual baseball player in mind — Dan Casey, who, though a pitcher, did manage to hit a big league home run (his only one) for the Philadelphia Phillies during the 1887 season. He was paid five dollars for the piece, which ends,

And somewhere men are laughing,
And somewhere children shout,
But there is no joy in Mudville —
Mighty Casey has struck out.

"Men seldom make passes at girls who wear glasses."
Dorothy Parker (1893–1967)

Feminist and author Dorothy Parker is best remembered for her caustic wit. It is said that when she heard about the death of Calvin Coolidge, she replied, "How can they tell?" The memorable quote regarding spectacles appears in her poem News Item, published in *Chant for Dark Hours* (1927). She first made her mark with verse (one of her early collections was entitled Enough Rope), but her accomplishments were not limited to poetry. She wrote screenplays, short fiction and dramatic criticism, and served as a foreign correspondent during the Spanish Civil War.

"You drive for show but putt for dough."
Bobby Locke (1917–1987)

One of the most epigrammatic phrases heard on the golf course, "You drive for show but putt for dough" originated with South African professional Bobby Locke, three-time winner of the PGA's Vardon Trophy for lowest scoring average. Widely regarded as one of the greatest putters ever, quipster Locke coined the phrase to deflect attention from the game's big hitters. It's a sentiment most golfers would echo.

CHAPTER 2
WHO REALLY SAID IT?

Quotations Often Erroneously Attributed

"God helps those who help themselves."
Attributed to the Bible

> This is probably the most quoted "biblical" passage that it is nowhere to be found in the Bible. It does appear several times in *Poor Richard's Almanack* (1733–1758), by Benjamin Franklin, who almost certainly popularized it. Earlier, in 1668, French poet Jean de la Fontaine wrote, "Help yourself and God will help you." But the saying was around long before that, a persistent proverb which, as many devout Christians argue, is the antithesis of Jesus' teaching. The saying is indeed ancient. The moral of one of Aesop's fables, Hercules and the Wagoner (c.580 BCE), is "The gods help them that help themselves," and Greek playwright Aeschylus (525–456 BCE) wrote, "God loves to help him who strives to help himself."

"No sooner said than done."
Attributed to Quintus Ennius (c.239–169 BCE)

> Only fragments remain of the works of Roman poet Quintus Ennius, but the phrase found in fragment 315

of his Annals (c.81 BCE) is quite clear. Annals was a collection of personal and historical occurrences, and Ennius' popularity gave him cause to write about infamous events. While he often receives credit for this expression, it is believed Ennius was quoting Roman general Publius Cornelius Scipio (237–183 BCE) who, upon his victory in the battle of Hama in 202 BCE, spoke to the vanquished Hannibal: "But to what end do I speak so? 'No sooner said than done'—So acts your man of worth."

"Look before you leap."
Attributed to Thomas Tusser (c.1524–1580)

Thomas Tusser, an English farmer and author of agricultural poetry, included this pithy folk aphorism in his 1557 work, Hundredth Good Pointes of Husbandrie, along with many other wise maxims and instructions on farming. In chapter 57, a man advises his single friend to marry, but cautions him, "Look ere thou leap." The phrase, however, was already in print, having appeared eleven years earlier in *The Proverbs of John Heywood* (1546), a gnomic poem.

"Fools rush in where angels fear to tread."
Attributed to William Shakespeare (1564–1616)

Many believe this quasi-religious quote derives from the Bible, and some attribute it to Shakespeare, but the original author is Alexander Pope (1688–1744). The great

English poet wrote this in his Essay on Criticism, Part III, in 1711. He is denouncing critics who have something to say about everything, even those things which will admit of no imperfection.

No place so sacred from such fops is barred,
Nor is Paul's church more safe than Paul's churchyard:
Nay, fly to altars; there they'll talk you dead;
For fools rush in where angels fear to tread.

"Born with a silver spoon in his mouth."
Attributed to Miguel de Cervantes (1547–1616)

Cervantes' masterpiece, *Don Quixote* (1605–1615), contains hundreds of proverbial sayings, at least two dozen of which are still in common use in English today. This quote can be found in Part II, Book IV, chapter 73. Quotation sources often credit Cervantes with originating the saying, but it dates at least as far as Roman writer Decimus Junius Juvenalis (c.60–c.140), better known as Juvenal. His Satire 13 contains what was likely an old saying even to him, Gallinae filius albae, which can be loosely translated as "fortunate son." The saying refers to someone who has no knowledge of the difficulties faced by those who are not well off.

"All that glitters is not gold."
Attributed to Miguel de Cervantes (1547–1616)

> The expression was popularized by Spanish writer Cervantes in Don Quixote, Part II, Book III, chapter 33, wherein Quixote's squire Sancho Panza attempts to justify his loyalty to the unstable Quixote. "If you don't think it fit to give me an island because I am a fool," Panza says, "I'll be so wise as to not care whether you do or no. 'Tis an old saying, the Devil lurks behind the cross. All is not gold that glisters." Variations of this popular adage appear in many languages around the globe.

"I'll turn over a new leaf."
Attributed to Miguel de Cervantes (1547–1616)

> *Don Quixote* is a classic satirical tale mocking chivalry and wealth. In practical terms, it is an account of one man's adventurous journey in search of destiny. In Part II, Book III, chapter 13, Sancho Panza, tiring of his master's delusions, contemplates leaving the Don's service by muttering this well known proverb to a fellow squire. The word leaf refers to a sheet of paper. Often credited with originating the saying, Cervantes was merely creating rustic dialogue when he had Panza utter it. In truth, the phrase appeared in print at least five years before Cervantes was born, in Union of the Noble and Illustre Famelies of Lancastre and York, better known as Hall's

Chronicle (1542), by English historian Edward Hall (died 1547). Describing the events of a battle, Hall wrote, "When they saw the Englishmen at the weakest, they turned the leaf and sang another song."

"A bird in the hand is worth two in the bush."
Attributed to Miguel de Cervantes (1547–1616)

This ancient proverb not only appears in the writings of Greek poet Theocritus (c.300–c.250 BCE), but in many books of folklore and sayings published before 1600. The earliest known example after the Greek, printed in a collection of English proverbs in the fifteenth century, appears as, "A birde in hond is better than thre in the wode." In Cervantes' Don Quixote, Part I, Book IV, chapter four, Quixote's master's wife commands his presence, and while he delays to see her until he wins a battle, his squire says,

A bird in the hand is worth two in the bush,
And he that will not when he may
When he would, he shall have nay.

"People who live in glass houses shouldn't throw stones."

Attributed to George Herbert (1593–1633)

A well-worn proverb, it appears as "Whose house is of glass, must not throw stones at another" in *Jacula Prudentum* (1640), by English poet and rector George Herbert. A slightly different version in Olio (1789), by English philologist Francis Grose (c.1731–1791), reads, "One who has a head of glass should never engage in throwing stones." However, the earliest known printed source of this now tired cliché is Troilus and Criseyde (1385), a lengthy narrative poem by Geoffrey Chaucer (c.1340–1400). From, "Who that hath an hed of verre, Fro cast of stones war hym in the werre!" the saying we know today has sprung. The proverb reminds us that if we criticize others, we are prone to be criticized in return.

"Charity begins at home."

Attributed to Sir Thomas Browne (1605–1682)

In Part II, section iv, of Religio Medici (1642), by English philosopher Sir Thomas Browne, the author explores the human penchant for charity, and says that with virtue and charity come regrets and peeves. He writes, "'Charity begins at home' is the voice of the world; yet is every man his greatest enemy, and, as it were, his own executioner." While many credit Sir Thomas with originating this saying, he was quoting an ancient proverb that can be traced as far back as the writings of Greek poet Theocritus (c.300–c.250 BCE). Roman playwright Terence (185–159 BCE) included the expression in Act IV, scene i, of his drama Andria, and variations may be found in English Works (c.1380) by religious reformer John Wycliffe (c.1320–1384) and many other early sources.

"Cleanliness is next to godliness."
Attributed to John Wesley (1703–1791)

The commonly heard saying, often though to be from the Bible, is frequently credited to English clergyman John Wesley, founder of the Methodist church. In a sermon entitled On Dress (c.1790), based on a biblical passage, Wesley said, "Neither this nor any text of scripture condemns neatness of apparel... Cleanliness is, indeed, next to godliness." However, nearly a century before Wesley was born, English philosopher Francis Bacon (1561–1626) published Advancement of Learning (1605), an introduction to an encyclopedia of all knowledge that he never completed. Book II of this monumental work states, "Cleaness of body was ever deemed to proceed from a due reverence to God."

"A penny saved is a penny earned."
Attributed to Benjamin Franklin (1706–1790)

> Most Americans have heard this saying attributed to Ben Franklin since their early childhood. It does appear in his *Poor Richard's Almanack*, but Franklin did not originate the saying. Scottish poet James Thomson (1700–1748) can be credited with producing the first known printed source, but even then he was obviously quoting an old proverb. In his poem, The Castle of Indolence (1748), Thomson describes a town where all its people accumulate their wealth.

> *"A penny savèd is a penny got"* —
> *Firm to this scoundrel maxim keepeth he,*
> *Ne of its rigour will he bate a jot,*
> *Till it has quenched his fire, and banished his pot.*

"This is adding insult to injuries."
Attributed to Edward Moore (1712–1757)

> Edward Moore was a British linen draper who had the good fortune to become a famous writer in his time. Although he is now all but forgotten, he published poems and fables and was most successful as a dramatist. His first comedy, *The Foundling* (1748), based on Samuel Richardson's epistolary novel Pamela: or Virtue Rewarded (1740), contained the oft-quoted line in Act V, scene v. However, the expression had existed since the first century, appearing in Fabulae Aesopiae by Roman

writer Phaedrus. His collection of five books, consisting of Aesop's fables told in verse form, contained the phrase Iniuriae qui addideris contumeliam, or "injustices added to insults," in Book V, chapter three.

"Don't shoot till you see the whites of their eyes."
Attributed to William Prescott (1726–1795)

While colonel William Prescott has often been credited with the quote, it was major general Israel Putnam (1718–1790), at the Battle of Bunker Hill, June 17, 1775, who is believed to have been the first to utter it. The order was passed on, along with several other orders, to the U.S. troops defending the hill outside Boston. After three assaults by the British, the Americans were forced to withdraw due to a scant supply of ammunition. Because the U.S. troops were able to hold on so long, the loss of the battle actually became a significant boost to American morale.

"That government is best which governs least."
Attributed to Thomas Jefferson (1743–1826)

According to conservative columnist William F. Buckley and others, Thomas Jefferson supposedly made this laissez-faire statement, but the phrase first appeared in print in Henry David Thoreau's landmark essay, *Civil Disobedience* (1849), a work that greatly influenced Mohandas K. Gandhi and other activists. However, Thoreau refers to the saying by enclosing it in quotation marks, indicating that it was a well known proverb in his day.

"Let them eat cake."
Attributed to Marie Antoinette (1755–1793)

The saying has long been erroneously attributed to Marie Antoinette, queen of France, who became a choice target for agitators during the revolution. To buttress support for the revolution, many slanderous stories were told about the royals and aristocrats, including Marie, wife of Louis XVI. It was said the queen asked why the masses were so violently opposed to Louis' reign. "They are hungry, my lady," was the reply. "The people have no bread!" To which Marie innocently said, "What, no bread? Then let them eat cake." The quote is actually translated from Qu'ils mangent de las brioche, literally meaning "Let them eat pastry." French philosopher Jean Jacques Rousseau (1712–1778) related the story in his memoirs, The Confessions, Book VI, which were published in the mid 1780s. The quotation was likely attributed to Marie Antoinette to justify her murder and ridicule her memory.

"Should auld acquaintance be forgot, and days of auld lang syne?"

Attributed to Robert Burns (1759–1796)

This beloved New Year's Eve song, often credited to Scottish poet Robert Burns, is, in fact, of unknown authorship. As a poet, Burns was deeply interested and involved in the common people. He was an active folklorist, a collector of old songs and melodies that, before they were written down, were preserved only by word of mouth from one generation to another. Sometime before 1793, Burns met an old man who sang two nostalgic verses. Burns immediately found the lyric to be both beautiful and remarkable, and set it down in writing. He then composed three more verses, but his verses are usually omitted from printed versions of the songs and are never sung on New Year's Eve. The great poet's influence is felt, however, through the melody of the song. Burns found the singer's tune to be rather mediocre, and he therefore substituted a tune for which he had already written another poem. Incidentally, in the Scottish dialect *auld lang syne* literally means "old long ago" or "old long since," and is a reference to what we colloquially call "the good old days."

"Blood is thicker than water."
Attributed to Josiah Tattnail (1795–1871)

Josiah Tattnail was a U.S. naval officer assigned to America's first Asian Pacific fleet. In 1850, he offered the famous remark upon being asked why he chose to join the French and British shelling Shanghai Harbor. Though usually interpreted as a heroic statement, it was in reality offered apologetically because of America's official policy of neutrality in China's colonial wars. An ancient proverb, the saying actually had appeared in print many times before Tattnail uttered it. The earliest known instance occurred in Troy Book by English poet John Lydgate (c.1370–1451) Written between 1412–1420, and finally published in 1513, the opus contained reverent tributes to the great poet Chaucer, and Book III contained these lines:

For naturelly blod will ay of kynde
Draw unto blod, wher he may it fynde.

"Survival of the fittest."
Attributed to Charles Darwin (1809–1882)

The proposition that only the strongest and most adaptable creatures will survive in nature is often credited to British scientist Charles Darwin, but the phrase did not originate with him and does not appear in his famous treatise, *On the Origin of Species* (1859). In fact, Darwin's theory of evolution represented exactly the opposite idea. Simply put, he proposed that those creatures that were best suited to their environment, regardless of their physical condition, would have the greatest likelihood of survival. The biggest, strongest, or fastest animals might actually die out in favor of the small, weak and slow ones. The important factor was not the animal's fitness but those traits that best suit it to its habitat. The phrase gained popularity, being used mainly as a basis to attack the theory, and later as an excuse for inhumane behavior on the part of nations at war.

"You can fool all the people some of the time and some of the people all the time, but you can not fool all the people all the time."

Attributed to Abraham Lincoln (1809–1865)

It has been supposed that Abraham Lincoln said this while campaigning for the U.S. senate against Stephen A. Douglas, September 8, 1858, during a debate in Illinois. The debates were exhaustively covered by the newspapers, and there is an extensive record of what was said by each man. The phrase did not appear in print for nearly forty years, when it showed up in Lincoln's Yarns and Stories (1895) by American writer Alexander McClure (1832–1901). However, during the debates Lincoln did say, "A house divided against itself cannot stand; I believe this government cannot endure permanently, half slave and half free." Lincoln lost the election to Douglas but gained such notoriety for his reasoned rhetoric that he was elected president in 1860.

" 'Tis better to have loved and lost than never to have loved at all."
Attributed to Alfred, Lord Tennyson (1809–1892)

The great English poet did indeed write these words, in his In *Memoriam* (1850), but he was not the first to do so. Scottish poet Thomas Campbell (1777–1844), chiefly remembered for his patriotic lyrics, is the true originator of this all-too-true maxim. While he did not write the exact words we know today, he created the form and pattern of the expression which was subsequently altered by later poets.

What though at my heart he has tilted,
What though I have met with a fall?
Better to be courted and jiltedThan never be courted at all.

"There's a sucker born every minute."
Attributed to Phineas Taylor Barnum (1810–1891)

Showman and impresario P. T. Barnum, one of America's greatest publicists, is said to have coined this phrase when asked by a reporter how he expected to attract crowds to his circus. Barnum replied that, with feeding elephants and transporting the performers and equipment around the country, this was the least of his worries. The remark was interpreted as belittling the sophistication of his audiences. Though Barnum denied saying anything of the kind, it's likely his competitors pounced on the phrase, corrupting it into its present form and publicizing it in the hope of disparaging the success Barnum & Bailey's traveling extravaganza, The Greatest Show on Earth. Late in life, Barnum told a friend that if he had believed what he supposedly said, he'd never have gone to such great lengths to find the curiosities for his museum or the acts for his shows. The phrase was the unofficial title of his biography, first published in 1855.

"A watched pot never boils."
Attributed to Elizabeth Cleghorn Gaskell (1810–1865)

English writer Elizabeth Gaskell was the author of several popular novels, the most famous of which was *Cranford* (1853), the tale of a small English town unraveled by the coming of the railway. She also published poetry and nonfiction, including what many consider to be the best biography of Charlotte Brontë. All her writings revealed a strong distaste for the hypocrisy that was part of Victorian society. Her novel *Mary Barton* (1848), in which the famous quote appears in chapter 31, was a bold indictment of contemporary labor conditions. While this proverbial saying had been in circulation for centuries,

Gaskell's novel is the earliest known printed source, and she often receives credit for originating this time-worn saying.

"Go west, young man."
Attributed to Horace Greeley (1811–1872)

Newspaperman and politician Horace Greeley, who is usually associated with this saying, gave full credit to the source when he reprinted it in his New-York Tribune. The original author, John Babsone Soule (1803–1886), first published it in an article in the Terra Haute (Indiana) Express in 1851, in which he said, "Go west, young man, and grow up with the country." Horace Greeley, a supporter of many progressive ideas, quoted Soule when he editorialized on the vast untapped resources of the American wilderness and urged his readers to go forth and expand the frontier.

"Beauty is in the eye of the beholder."
Attributed to Margaret Wolfe Hungerford (c.1855–1902)

Molly Bawn, a novel published in 1878, is the story of a beautiful young girl named Eleanor (nicknamed Molly Bawn) who falls in love with a man she cannot marry because of his inadequate income. At one point, Molly's scheming and jealous cousin, Marcia, discusses Molly with Lady Stafford, a visitor. The lady comments that she heard Molly was beautiful, and Marcia answers with this ageless truth, insinuating she does not believe Molly is beautiful at all. While this wise aphorism had been spoken for generations, Hungerford's novel is the earliest known printed source.

"Build a better mousetrap and the world will beat a path to your door."
Attributed to Elbert Hubbard (1856–1915)

Prolific writer and newspaperman Elbert Hubbard claimed this common-sense quotation was original with him, while his opponents insisted it came from the eloquent utterances of New England essayist, Transcendentalist and Unitarian minister Ralph Waldo Emerson (1803–1882). The controversy surrounding the true authorship of this popular expression was one of the longest lived and most heated legal battles in the history of the Unites States. The issue flared up in 1889, when diarist Sarah Y. B. Yule (1856–1916) credited the quote to Emerson in her Borrowings, spurring Hubbard to make his claim as the original author. Finally, in 1912, to quiet the controversy surrounding the issue, Yule made a public announcement stating she had copied the quotation into her personal handbook directly from a lecture given by Emerson. The actual quote reads as follows: "If a man write a better book, preach a better sermon, or make a better mousetrap than his neighbor, though he build his house in his woods, the world will beat a path to his door." Despite the outcome of the controversy, the quotation is still, on occasion, credited to Elbert Hubbard.

"All I know is what I read in the papers."
Attributed to Will Rogers (1879–1935)

The quotation is invariably attributed to American comic and writer Will Rogers, whose homespun sense of humor was sharpest when deriding the politicians of his day and exposing the vagaries of current events. He usually began his monologue in the Ziegfeld Follies with some variation of, "Well, all I know is just what I read in the newspapers." But Rogers did not coin the phrase. Instead he heard it from eminent journalist Herbert Bayard Swope (1882–1958), a foreign correspondent during World War I. Swope framed the statement as a serious reply to a question about the source of his own seemingly limitless fund of information. Rogers was taken by Swope's answer and made it a staple of his act.

"The buck stops here."
Attributed to Harry S Truman (1884–1972)

While president Harry S Truman is credited with originating the saying, he didn't. It was a quote he lived by, and it was a quote associated with his presidency, but it was a quote inscribed on a plaque that sat on his White House desk. Truman received the plaque as a commemoration of his visit to an eastern university while he was a U.S. senator. The saying derives from the phrase pass the buck, meaning blame someone else, but Truman was noted for his willingness to accept responsibility for his actions and the actions of his subordinates.

"If you can't stand the heat, get out of the kitchen."
Attributed to Harry S Truman (1884–1972)

The remark is also associated with president Truman, who faced a major crisis every day of his presidency, but when he said it, he was quoting his life-long friend and presidential military aide, general Harry Hawkins Vaughan (1893–1981). Vaughan was a cigar chomping Falstaffian character and the most criticized associate of a much-criticized president. Truman and Vaughan would host poker games in the White House with potential appointees, during which Vaughan would mercilessly rip the candidates. If they got too flustered or couldn't take the ribbing, Truman felt they weren't suitable for appointment to office. Despite the fact that Vaughan was a troublemaker and an endless source of grief for the president, Truman never wavered in his loyalty to his old World War I pal. In fact, he even seemed to relish the way the general would irritate not only the senate and the press, but the rest of the White House staff.

CHAPTER 3
WHAT WAS ACTUALLY SAID?

Quotations Often Misquoted

"There but for the grace of God go I."
John Bradford (c.1510–1555)

> When British religious leader John Bradford saw a group of criminals being led to their execution, he actually said, "But for the grace of God there goes John Bradford." Chaplain to King Edward VI (1537-1553), Bradford was accused of sedition by the king's successor, his elder half-sister Mary (1516–1558). Condemned as a heretic, he and some 290 other Protestant martyrs perished under the persecution of the Catholic monarch labeled "Bloody Mary" prior to modern revisionist accounts of her eventful life and tragic death.

"Music hath charms to soothe the savage beast."
William Congreve (1670–1729)

> British playwright William Congreve penned *The Mourning Bride* in 1697, in which the famous quote appears in Act I, Scene 1. In Congreve's tragedy, the title character mourns the death of the king of Valencia in Spain, who

has been buried in Granada as a captive. The king is secretly her father-in-law, and her husband is presumed dead as well. The bride says,

Musick has Charms to sooth a savage Breast,
To soften Rocks, or bend a knotted Oak.
I've read, that things inanimate have moved,
And, as with living Souls, have been informed,
By Magick Numbers and persuasive Sound.

The quotation is frequently heard as, "Music hath charms to soothe the savage beast," which, though technically inaccurate, conveys a similar meaning.

"Nothing is easy for a dying man."
Benjamin Franklin (1706–1790)

Ben Franklin uttered these dying words after his doctor advised him to turn on his side to make breathing easier. "A dying man can do nothing easily" was his reply. Franklin died on April 17, 1790, three months into his 84th year.

"Nothing is certain but death and taxes."
Benjamin Franklin (1706–1790)

Benjamin Franklin is famous for so many things, not least of which are the hundreds of colorful aphorisms he popularized in his *Poor Richard's Almanack* during the mid-eighteenth century. His most enduring remarks were made as an octogenarian during the great debates of the framers of the U.S. Constitution. The famous remark, now one of the most widely used clichés in American discourse, traces its origin to a speech written by the ailing Dr. Franklin before final ratification of the constitution. The complete excerpt reads, "Our new constitution is now established and has an appearance that promises permanency; but in this world nothing can be said to be certain but death and taxes."

"Master of all he surveys."
William Cowper (1731–1800)

Scottish sailor Alexander Selkirk (1676–1721), following a rancorous quarrel with his captain, was cast ashore alone on a desert island where he was marooned five years. His adventure became the basis for Daniel Defoe's novel, *Robinson Crusoe* (1719). British poet William Cowper (pronounced "Cooper") penned the following lines in 1782 on behalf of the unfortunate seaman, who longs for home and human contact.

I am monarch of all I survey,
My right there is not to dispute;
From the centre all round to the sea,
I am lord of the fowl and the brute.

"The best laid plans of mice and men often go astray."

Robert Burns (1759–1796)

Robert Burns, the son of a farmer, wrote most of his poetry in the country idiom and dialect of Scots-English. Throughout his works he displays a great love for all the creatures of the earth, even the very humblest. The famous line is found in his short poem, *To a Mouse: On Turning Her Up in Her Nest with the Plough.* The poet is sorry to have disturbed the mouse and mutters,

But, Mousie, thou art no thy lane [not alone],
In proving foresight may be vain;
The best laid schemes o' mice an' men
Gang aft a-gley.

"I regret that I have but one life to give my country."

Nathan Hale (1755–1776)

A school teacher commissioned in the Connecticut militia, Nathan Hale achieved martyrdom after being summarily hanged as a spy by the British during the American Revolutionary War. His fame is largely the consequence of his last words, attributed to him by a British colonel who was impressed by the young man's patriotic zeal. In a statement before being executed on September 22, 1776, Hale reportedly said, "I only regret that I have but one life to lose for my country." The statement quickly became an inspiration for the rebellious colonists.

"A sharp tongue grows sharper with constant use."
Washington Irving (1783–1859)

"Time grew worse and worse with Rip Van Winkle as years of matrimony rolled on; a tart temper never mellows, and a sharp tongue is the only edged tool that grows sharper with constant use." Thus wrote American author Washington Irving in describing "the furnace of domestic tribulation" that his most famous character escaped by his twenty-year-long snooze. The sharp tongue belonged to Van Winkle's wife, whose knack for complaining was matched only by her husband's knack for avoiding gainful employment. The expression was popularized by Joseph Jefferson, who played Rip Van Winkle for almost forty years in a traveling dramatization of the story following the U.S. Civil War.

"A woman of a certain age."
George Gordon Byron (1788–1824)

Although this quote is usually associated with the French male and his eminently sensible appreciation for middle-aged women, it was British poet Lord Byron, no slacker in his appreciation for women of all ages, who penned these well known words. In stanza 22 of his satire *Beppo* (1817), Byron describes Laura, whose husband and lover sort out their differences over coffee.

She was not old, nor young,
nor at the years
which people call a certain age,
which yet the most uncertain age appears.

"There's an exception to every rule."
Margaret Fuller (1810–1850)

Author and social reformer Margaret Fuller was one of the most forward-thinking women of the nineteenth century. Her writings constitute some of the earliest examples of feminist thought. She founded the Boston Conversationalists in 1838, a club wherein women engaged in lively discussions on all the important issues of the day. An intimate of Oliver Wendell Holmes, Amos Bronson Alcott and Ralph Waldo Emerson, she was also an active Transcendentalist. She was the founding editor of The Dial, the primary organ of Transcendentalism, where her many essays espoused the pursuit of freedom, reason and the democratic process. The well known quote, as it appears in her 1843 essay, *The Great Lawsuit, Man Versus Men, Woman Versus Women*, was originally written, "Nature provides exceptions to every rule."

"The best is yet to come."
Robert Browning (1812–1889)

Deriving from the poem *Rabbi Ben Ezra* (1864), English poet Robert Browning instills hope in the aging with this commonly heard, but often misquoted, phrase. Refuting the belief that youth is the best time of life, the rabbi explains that life is a growing process, that God wants life to thrive and develop as time goes on. Instead of wallowing in the concept of age, the rabbi encourages the world to drink life in, saying, "Grow old along with me! The best is yet to be."

"All is fair in love and war."
Ellen Wood (1813–1887)

When the saying appeared in Ellen Wood's novel, East Lynne, the line was, "All stratagems are fair in love and war." When the novel was adapted into a play, the character Levison spoke those exact words in Act III, scene ii. Through time, however, stratagems have commonly been dropped in favor of the simpler and more direct pronouncement we know today.

"Give him enough rope and he will hang himself."
Charlotte Brontë (1816–1855)

> In a political debate between a Whig and a Tory, Mr. Moore, the Whig, exclaims, "If I judged them, I'd give them short shrift! ...but I mean to let them quite alone in this bout, to give them rope enough, certain that in the end they will hang themselves." Charlotte Brontë's novel, *Shirley* (1847), in which the original quote appears in chapter three, involves several debates between Moore and his Tory opponent Mr. Helstone. Over time, the true quote has metamorphosed into the short but powerful saying we now frequently hear.

"It's like playing tennis without a net."
Robert Frost (1874–1963)

> Robert Frost, who captured perhaps more than any other American poet the love and admiration of common and uncommon readers alike, was also reckoned to be one of the meanest men who ever lived by those who knew him, especially other poets. What he actually said, in a reference to writing blank verse, was, "I'd rather play tennis with the net down" (Newsweek, 1961).

"Rose is a rose is a rose."
Gertrude Stein (1874–1946)

One of the most controversial writers of the twentieth century, Gertrude Stein's best-known quote is often heard incorrectly as, "A rose is a rose is a rose." However, she is not speaking about a flower, but a person. The line appears in her 1913 novel, *Sacred Emily*. Stein's literary achievements may be questionable, but during her career she wrote novels, plays, verse, prose poems and even an opera, and she was one of the first writers to experiment with the non-narrative style associated with her close friend Ernest Hemingway.

"I must go down to the sea again."
John Masefield (1878–1957)

This is the opening line of John Masefield's most popular poem, *Sea Fever* (1902). When Masefield became England's poet laureate he unfortunately felt obliged to write everything in verse. "I must go down to the sea again" is the way the line is most often quoted, but it is not the way it is usually printed. "I must go down to the seas again" is the way it first appeared in print, but this was a typographical error. In spite of Masefield's attempts to correct later reprints, the error persisted. However, most people remember the line the way the poet wanted it.

I must go down to the sea again, to the lonely sea and the sky,
And all I ask is a tall ship and a star to steer her by.

"That's one small step for man, one giant leap for mankind."

Neil Armstrong (1930– 2013)

It was July 21, 1969, when this famous U.S. astronaut stepped down from the ladder of the lunar module Eagle to become the first human being to walk on the moon. Uncounted millions watching the event on television or listening on the radio heard him say, "That's one small step for man." They did not hear the carefully prepared phrase, "for a man." Armstrong later stated that he had not flubbed the message and had properly said "a man," but that the immense distance and radio static had erased the small word for the listening audience.

"Play it again, Sam."

Attributed to Humphrey Bogart in Casablanca (1942);
Screenplay by Julius J. Epstein, et. al.

Though it's one of the most celebrated lines in motion picture history, film devotees are astonished to learn that "Play it again, Sam" is never actually said in Casablanca, the popular film starring Humphrey Bogart and Ingrid Bergman. Set in French Morocco in the midst of World War II, Bogart plays American nightclub owner Rick Blaine, who is trying to forget the pain of Ilse, his unrequited love. He has given a standing order to Sam, the house pianist, never to play a certain song that was always Ilse's favorite. Soon, however, events unexpectedly bring Ilse to Casablanca, and one night she appears at Rick's Café Américain. Not finding Rick there, Ilse says to the pianist, "Play it once, Sam, for old time's sake." Sam, played characteristically by Dooley Wilson, reluctantly agrees, but the song attracts Rick's attention and he puts a stop to it. Later, after closing for the night, Rick and Sam are the only two people in the café. Rick says, "You played it for her, you can play it for me." When Sam protests, Rick becomes insistent. "If she can stand it, I can. Play it!" Incidentally, the film contains many popular remarks that have become popularly known, among them: "Here's looking at you kid;" "This is the start of a beautiful friendship;" "Of all the gin joints in the world, she had to walk into mine."

CHAPTER 4
WHAT WAS REALLY MEANT?

Quotations Often Misunderstood

"Might makes right."
Plato (427–347 BCE)

> Plato's monumental work *The Republic* (c.375 BCE) is a
> dialogue between Socrates and a group of multi-syllabic
> poet-philosophers named Simonides, Thrasymachus,
> Adeimantus and Glaucon. Book I begins with the ques-
> tion, "What is justice?" Adeimantus says, "I proclaim
> that might is right, justice the interest of the stronger."
> The others similarly argue that justice is a matter of self
> interest, expediency and whatever you can get away
> with—all of which sound suspiciously like injustice. Soc-
> rates, however, finally manages to show them that justice
> does not always bring rewards, but must be pursued for
> its own sake. The saying, "Might makes right," originally
> intended as a spur toward justice, is now often used as
> an excuse for pursuing inequality and injustice.

"Spare the rod and spoil the child."
Samuel Butler (1612–1680)

> This familiar proverb is often thought to be from the
> Bible, but in reality, it was English poet Samuel Butler's

Hudibras (1663) in which the saying first occurs. In Part II, Sir Hudibras, the English equivalent of Don Quixote, and his squire, Ralpho, are imprisoned. Hudibras proposes marriage to a widow, who agrees to free him and marry him only if he will endure a whipping, an action men once fared for their lovers as a sign of purity and virtue. She supports this ritual, saying,

Love is a boy, by poets styled,
Then spare the rod, and spoil the child.

A similar expression occurs in the Bible: "He that spareth his rod, hateth his son" (Proverbs 13:24), but the meaning is far removed from the circumstances in Butler's poem. Now heard as an excuse to behave harshly towards children, the original intent of the line was that love deserved to be tested before entering into marriage.

"Full of the milk of human kindness."
William Shakespeare (1564–1616)

This agreeable phrase was not intended as a compliment by the murderous Lady Macbeth. Her greatest fear, as revealed in her soliloquy in Act I, scene v, was that her husband might not be willing to "play false" and step into the role of king.

Yet do I fear thy nature;
It is too full o' the milk of human kindness
To catch the nearest way.

Now a tired cliché, the phrase gradually acquired its pleasant associations with the help of eighteenth century writers like Charles Churchill: "With the sweet milk of human kindness blessed, the furious ardour of my zeal repressed." and Edmund Burke: "These gentle historians dip their pens in nothing but the milk of human kindness."

"In one fell swoop."
William Shakespeare (1564–1616)

As the tragedy plays out, Macbeth has sought to secure the royal succession for his own line by murdering his rival, Macduff, and his family. Macbeth's henchmen surprise and murder Macduff's wife and children. In Act IV, Scene iii, Macduff responds to the terrible news with disbelief:

All my pretty ones?
Did you say all? O hell kite! All?
What, all my pretty chickens and their dam
At one fell swoop?

Those who regularly use this catch phrase with the meaning, roughly, of "with one shot," or "in one motion," are probably not aware of the archaic meaning of fell, which is a cousin of the word felon and means "ruthless" or "savage."

"O Romeo, Romeo! wherefore art thou Romeo?"
William Shakespeare (1564–1616)

In Act II of William Shakespeare's *Romeo and Juliet* (1597), Juliet is not yelling for Romeo; she is not beckoning, hearkening nor commandeering him, as is often thought by those who repeat this popular quote. Juliet is in love with Romeo, but the two come from enemy families, making a nice get-together with their parents rather difficult. In the scene, Juliet stands on the ever-present balcony, talking to herself of her woeful love, asking aloud, not "where" is Romeo, but "wherefore [why] is Romeo?" Why is he a member of the family she is honor bound to despise?

O Romeo, Romeo! wherefore art thou Romeo?
Deny thy father, and refuse thy name;
Or, if thou wilt not, be but sworn my love,
And I'll no longer be a Capulet.

"First we kill all the lawyers."
William Shakespeare (1564–1616)

There is probably no phrase in Shakespeare that is so often used in the wrong context. In *Henry VI, Part 2* (1598), devious Jack Cade and his followers muse upon what would have to be done to destabilize society, to make a revolution and allow a despot to take control. The comment is not a condemnation of lawyers; in fact,

Shakespeare uses the statement as the highest compliment for lawyers. The only thing standing in the way of Cade's execution of his corrupt ideas is the lawyers, the protectors of a democratic society.

"There shall be no love lost."
Ben Jonson (1572–1637)

English dramatist Ben Jonson's second play, *Every Man Out of His Humour* (1600), was a brilliant satire that poked fun at several leading playwrights of the day and caused a feud known as the "War of the Theatres." In the play, three characters named Brisk, Buffone, and Sogliardo joke about turning horses into toys. Buffone changes the subject slightly by joking that Brisk is in love with Sogliardo, whereupon Sogliardo says, "There shall be no love lost." The original intention of the line was to indicate that Sogliardo felt the same toward Brisk, but today the same phrase means the opposite; that love is not an option.

"He had the Midas touch."
Richard Lassels (1603–1668)

In Greek mythology, the gods granted the wish of Midas, legendary king of ancient Phrygia, who asked that everything he touched be turned to gold. It was a foolish wish and its fulfillment became a curse, for even the very food Midas tried to eat turned to gold before he could consume it. What was originally meant to be a curse is now applied as a compliment to business promoters and financiers. The idea that the "Midas touch" is a blessing, even an endowment of genius, traces back to *The Voyage of Italy* by Richard Lassels, who wrote of Italian painter and architect Raphael (1483–1520), that his "touch of a finger could, Midas like, turn galley pots to gold."

"When in Rome, do as the Romans do."
Jeremy Taylor (1613–1667)

The expression first appeared in English theologian Jeremy Taylor's religious publication *Ductor Dubitantium* (1660). His phrase, "If you are in Rome, live in the Roman style," was originally meant to support his assertion that if all people followed God's commands there would be no cultural differences between peoples, and the misunderstandings caused by contradicting customs would vanish. However, the expression is used today with quite the opposite meaning, reminding us to be more tolerant and understanding of the ways of others.

"Hell hath no fury like a woman scorned."
William Congreve (1670–1729)

William Congreve's witty Restoration comedy, *The Way of the World* (1700), has a complex plot involving deceptive suitors, virtuous coquettes, reformed rakes, secret affairs, threatened divorces and lots of longing for love.

In Act III, scene viii, the rejected Lady Wishfort ("wish for it") says,

Heaven has no rage like love to hatred turned,
Nor hell a fury like a woman scorned.

Ironically, a few scenes earlier, the same character says, "A little disdain is not amiss. A little scorn is alluring." Today, the insincere, coquettish nature of the quotation is almost completely forgotten.

"A little learning is a dangerous thing."
Alexander Pope (1688–1744)

In his *Essay on Criticism* (1711), Alexander Pope likens criticism of poetry to overindulging in drinks that "intoxicate the brain." Those who are not clever enough for such sentiments, the great poet avers, are like drunks not able to carry their drink. A universal quote, now proverbial, it was originally meant as a warning to those who might deprecate fine poetry. Today, it is usually heard as a terse command to cease questioning and be satisfied with ignorance.

"Damn the torpedoes, full speed ahead!"
David Glasgow Farragut (1801–1870)

Naval commodore David G. Farragut gave this famous order on August 5, 1864, during the battle for Mobile Bay in the Civil War. When warned by his navigator of the danger, the commodore exclaimed, "Damn the torpedoes! Captain Drayton, go ahead." While Farragut's name is commonly associated with the saying, it is not well known that during this era, the term torpedo was used to describe an underwater or floating mine.

"I hear you loud and clear."
Lewis Carroll (1832–1898)

The slogan became commonplace with the advent of the "walkie talkie" (mobile radio) during World War II, when the sender needed assurance that his messages were being heard. In truth, the original saying was used with just the reverse meaning—a declaration that one's message had been vigorously delivered. The saying originated in English author Lewis Carroll's allegory Through the Looking Glass (1872), in which Humpty Dumpty states, "I said it loud and clear; I went and shouted in his ear."

"Let the punishment fit the crime."
Sir William S. Gilbert (1836–1911)

The oft-heard quote originated in Act II of the satirical operetta The Mikado (1885). In this most formal of Gilbert and Sullivan's musical dramas, the Mikado of Japan pontificates a rigid moral code for his people. He is disappointed on behalf of the newest executioner, Ko-Ko,

at the total lack of customers. Ko-Ko, incidentally, is under penalty of death for flirting. Facetiously reminding
the audience that he is a compassionate ruler and en-
deavors to decree a punishment that is appropriate to
the offense it seeks to redress, the Mikado sings,

My object all sublime
I shall achieve in time—
To let the punishment fit the crime—
The punishment fit the crime;
And make each prisoner pent
Unwillingly represent
A source of innocent merriment!
Of innocent merriment.

"Good fences make good neighbors."
Robert Frost (1874–1963)

In Robert Frost's poem, *Mending Wall* (1914), two neigh-
boring farmers walk along their fence in springtime. The
narrator is feeling playful and makes a few light-hearted
jokes. The other farmer, somewhat more practical, responds with the famous quotation. Today, many repeat
the line and ascribe the saying directly to Frost without
realizing he didn't agree with the sentiment; he actually
thought that the farmer uttering the remark was unnec-
essarily stodgy.

"And I don't mean maybe."
Gus Kahn (1886–1941)

Those who use this catch phrase with a severe or menacing tone, and assume that the matter is deadly serious and the implied threat something dire, will be surprised to hear of the phrase's origin in a spirited but nonviolent vaudeville song of 1922, Yes, Sir, That's My Baby by Gus Kahn and composer Walter Donaldson. The tune was made popular by the leading entertainer of the day, Al Jolson. Kahn's lyric begins,

Yes, sir, that's my baby.
No, sir, I don't mean maybe.
Yes, sir, that's my baby now.

CHAPTER 5
WHY WAS IT SAID?

Quotations in Their Original Context

"One good turn deserves another."
Petronius (died c.66)

In Roman writer Petronius' prose satirical romance, *The Satyricon*, section 45, idle chatter follows a feast in the house of a noble who has retired for the evening. His guests discuss an upcoming gladiatorial spectacle. Echion, a clothing merchant, complains of the quality of the action. He explains that he clapped for a performance by Norbanus and insinuated that his applause was more than Norbanus' performance warranted, because in a past match, the gladiators fought badly. "Reckon it up," Echion says, "and I gave you more than I got. One good turn deserves another."

"You have hit the nail on the head."
François Rabelais (1495–1553)

In the five-part satirical work *Gargantua and Pantagruel* (1532–1564), a collection of allegories featuring fantastic characters and places by French humorist François Rabelais, a friend of Pantagruel cannot decide if he should marry. He eventually accepts the advice of a physician who discourages him. Muttering in agreement, he says, "It is not very inexpedient that I marry, and that I should not care for being a cuckold. You have there hit the nail on the head." The expression wormed its way into English vernacular due to its frequent use by British general Johnny Burgoyne (1722–1792), who was fond of saying it to his troops during shooting practice. Forced to give up a life devoted to the stage, Burgoyne took his love for drama onto the battlefield during the American Revolution. After he surrendered at Saratoga, New York, in 1777, Burgoyne happily resumed his vocation England, publishing The Heiress (1786), in which the popular expression appears in Act III.

"Knowledge is power."
Francis Bacon (1561–1626)

The quotation first appeared in English theologian Francis Bacon's infamous essay *Of Heresies* in 1597. Now an "information age" mantra, the phrase originated in quite a different context. In writing of heresy, Bacon believed that those heresies which denied or limited the power of God were the most offensive. In particular, he argued that those who believed in the free will of Man, as opposed to predestination, were really denying God's power, "for knowledge is itself power," while the heretics reduce God to "an unconcerned looker on."

"The face that launched a thousand ships."
Christopher Marlow (1564–1593)

The medieval legend of Faust, who sold his soul to the devil, was brought to the Elizabethan stage in Christopher Marlow's *The Tragical History of Dr. Faustus*. When the demon Mephistopheles presents Faustus with Helen of Troy, the most beautiful woman in the legendary world, Faustus is reminded of the ancient war waged by Spartan king Menelaus to recapture Helen. Faustus asks,

Was this the face that launched a thousand ships,
And burnt the topless towers of Ilium?

"I'm all ears."
John Milton (1608–1674)

The saying, meaning, "I'm listening carefully," was phrased "I was all ear" in English poet John Milton's masque *Comus* (1637). In the story, an earl's two sons and daughter walk through a woods, and as the daughter tires, the sons separate to find food for her. A shepherd warns them that an evil wizard rules the area and turns trespassers into beasts. The shepherd, who is actually the wizard's attendant in disguise, tells the brothers the wizard had been talking to their sister, but that he listened in on the conversation.

I was all ear,
And took in strains that might create a soul
Under the ribs of death.

"No time like the present."
Mary de la Rivière Manley (1663–1724)

While English political writer Mary de la Rivière Manley's play *The Lost Lover* (1696) did not fare well at the theater—audiences did not approve of her adulterous lifestyle, prison record and slander of Whigs—her phrase stands the test of time. In Act IV, Lady Young-Love, a haughty woman with a daughter the object of several men's desires, and Sir Amourous Courtall, whose name is self-explanatory, engage in a witty conversation. When Lady Young-Love thinks she cannot compliment him the way he has wooed her, Sir Amourous delivers the famous quotation to encourage her to seize the moment.

"Take care of the minutes, for the hours will take care of themselves."
Philip Dormer Stanhope, Lord Chesterfield (1694–1773)

English statesman, essayist and epigramist Lord Chesterfield was one of the most important authors of the eighteenth century. He was devoted to his son, Philip (1732–1768), who was born illegitimately but overcame that social stigma to become a member of parliament like his father. In 1774, Lord Chesterfield's widow, the Duchess of Kendal, published her late husband's correspondence as Letters to his Son, containing descriptions of the manners and standards of a man of the world and an entertaining variety of shrewd and witty observations. Chesterfield wrote the famous statement to Philip in an attempt to bring him out of a slump and remind him not to let precious moments to go to waste.

"That's another story."
Laurence Sterne (1713–1768)

From 1759 to 1767, British novelist Laurence Sterne published nine volumes of *The Life and Opinions of Tristram Shandy*. In Book II, four men engage in a lively discussion interspersed with readings. When corporal Trim begins reciting a segment on the Inquisition, he remembers his brother, who was imprisoned in Portugal. Trim becomes so flustered he interrupts himself several times, saying, "That's another story," thus dismissing parts of the reading without letting on that there is more to it than his companions realize.

"Ask me no questions, and I'll tell you no lies."
Oliver Goldsmith (1728–1774)

In the play, *She Stoops to Conquer* (1773), the character Tony Lumpkin is overjoyed in hearing that Mr. Hastings wants to elope with Miss Neville, who Lumpkin's mother wants him to marry. Lumpkin even goes so far as to steal his mother's jewels to help the couple finance their plan. When asked how he managed to get hold of the jewels, a guilty Lumpkin delivers the popular saying, hinting that if the issue is not mentioned, he will not be obliged to invent a falsehood.

"Not much worse for wear."
William Cowper (1731–1800)

William Cowper was a minor British poet who wrote course and humorous verse. "Not much worse for wear" is found in his comic ballad, *The Diverting History of John Gilpin* (1782), and refers to the hat worn by the main character. In the story, Gilpin's borrowed mount suddenly and inexplicably gallops off in frenzy, damaging Gilpin's hat. After a bizarre adventure, Gilpin returns the horse to its owner, who presents Gilpin with his damaged hat. Though the hat is in no condition to be worn, Gilpin accepts it gladly, delivering the famous line. Cowper is best known for authoring the hymn God Moves in a Mysterious Way in 1779.

"What has posterity done for us?"
Sir Boyle Roche (1743–1807)

Irishman Sir Boyle Roche, member of the British parliament, offered the immortal quotation in answer to a member of parliament who thundered, "And what shall we do for posterity?" Sir Boyle is reputed to be the original target of the saying, "Every time he opens his mouth he puts his foot in it." Called "our delicious buffoon" by king George III, Sir Boyle's sublime absurdities uttered during parliamentary debate are legendary. "Half the lies our opponents tell about us are not true!" he is said to have declared during a particularly riotous session. Two of his most famous quotes were "I smell a rat, I see him floating in the air, but mark me, I shall nip him in the bud!" and that England and Ireland "are two sisters who should embrace like one brother."

"Out of sight is out of mind."
Johann Wolfgang von Goethe (1749–1832)

The line is from Part I, scene xii, of German poet Goethe's famous play Faust. Ironically, the speaker, Gretchen (Margarete), will indeed be out of her mind in a few more scenes. The popular proverbial sentiment is exactly the opposite of "Absence makes the heart grow fonder," another oft-repeated platitude. Incidentally, the quote was once used to demonstrate the difficulty of programming computers to perform the delicate task of translation. The phrase, "Out of sight, out of mind," was run through a computer program designed to translate English into Russian. When the translation was completed, the resulting Russian phrase was then run through a program that translated Russian into Chinese.

In the final step of the process, the Chinese phrase was translated back into English and came out as "Invisible, insane."

"Peter Piper picked a peck of pickled peppers."
Attributed to J. Harris (1763–1830)

The most popular tongue twister in the English language first appeared in print in London, published by school instructor J. Harris. It is not certain whether Harris wrote these lines, but it is known that he published a series of books for young readers known as *Harris's Cabinet*. In a little booklet entitled *Peter Piper's Practical Principles of Plain and Perfect Pronunciation* (1803), an entire alphabet of rhymes appeared. Peter Piper was unquestionably the most popular character of the bunch, but Kimbo Kemble, Oliver Oglethorpe and Tip-Toe Tommy certainly had their admirers. Each rhyme followed the same four-line pattern, with a statement followed by two questions:

Peter Piper picked a Peck of Pickled Peppers:
Did Peter Piper pick a Peck of Pickled Peppers?
If Peter Piper picked a Peck of Pickled Peppers,
Where's the Peck of Pickled Peppers Peter Piper picked?

"You'll be damned if you do and damned if you don't."
Lorenzo Dow (1777–1834)

In 1832, American religious leader Lorenzo Dow wrote Reflections on the Love of God, an early meditation manual. Dow spent his life traveling the world and preaching the gospel before returning to the United States. In the book, Dow mocks preachers who speak of conflicting interpretations of the Bible, who say,

'You can and you can't— You shall and you shan't—
You will and you won't—
And you will be damned it you do—
And you will be damned if you don't.'

"That's chicken feed!"
Davy Crockett (1786–1836)

The expression, meaning "small change," was first used by congressman Davy Crockett to describe the profits of small-time riverboat gamblers. Crockett, famous in the East for his colorful backwoods language, described the ways of the professionals as they fleeced the green-horns, noting that as small-town suckers had precious little money to lose, the gambling take was minimal. To him, the gamblers were merely "picking up chicken feed." As a former farmer and frontiersman, Crockett knew from first hand experience that chickens are fed scrap and seeds unfit for any other purpose.

"It was six of one and half a dozen of the other."
Frederick Marryat (1792–1848)

English naval captain Frederick Marryat wrote many novels about ships and the lives of sailors. In *The Pirate* (1836), sailors on a ship from New Orleans bound for Liverpool discuss their plans for their time ashore. One sailor, Bill, decides he will marry, and while the sailors harp about his womanizing past, the famous comment occurs. Hinting there is no difference, despite appearances, between two similar situations, the sailors chide Bill that he will still be a womanizer after he takes the plunge.

"There's no getting blood out of a turnip."
Frederick Marryat (1792–1848)

One of Frederick Marryat's most popular novels was *Japhet in Search of a Father* (1836). Japhet, preparing for a future as a doctor, and a boy named Timothy, begin apprenticing for an apothecary. Japhet first learns how to draw blood from a cabbage leaf before his mentor lets him use his arm, and Timothy mutters the popular saying, continuing, "but it seems there is more chance with a cabbage."

"The shot heard round the world."
Ralph Waldo Emerson (1803–1882)

Ralph Waldo Emerson's immortal line is now used principally by sports reporters to describe dramatic home runs or holes-in-one. In the final inning of the final game of the National League playoffs in 1951, Robert "Bobby" Thompson's three-run homer won the pennant for the New York Giants. It was universally hailed as "the shot heard round the world." The original, however, had nothing to do with athletics. It appeared in Emerson's *Concord Hymn* (1837), a poem written to celebrate the second battle of the American War of Independence:

By the rude bridge that arched the flood,
Their flag to April's breeze unfurled,
Here once the embattled farmers stood,
And fired the shot heard round the world.

"This is war."
Charles Francis Adams (1807–1886)

American historian and railroad commissioner Charles Francis Adams (1835–1915) penned a biography his famous father in *Life of Charles Francis Adams* (1900). The senior Adams was to keep Britain neutral during the U.S. Civil War, and upon hearing that England had built two iron rams for the confederacy, a series of letters ensued between him and Lord John Russell (1792–1878), the

British foreign secretary. After several fruitless exchanges, Adams sent Lord Russell an inflammatory letter that finally led to seizure of the weapons. Adams' letter, which was later reprinted in his biography, contains the blatant comment, "It would be superfluous in me to point out to your lordship that this is war."

"With malice toward none and charity for all."
Abraham Lincoln (1809–1865)

Excerpted from Lincoln's second inaugural address in March 1865, these memorable words sought to calm the passions of militant unionists bent on exacting revenge on the South for igniting the U.S. Civil War in 1861. The complete sentence is worthy of repetition: "With malice toward none, with charity for all, with firmness in the right as God gives us to see the right, let us strive on to finish the work we are in, to bind up the nation's wounds, to care for him who shall have borne the battle, and for his widow and his orphan, to do all which may achieve and cherish a just and lasting peace among ourselves and with all nations."

"A man's reach should exceed his grasp or what's a heaven for?"
Robert Browning (1812–1889)

In *Andrea del Sarto* (1855), a dramatic monologue, English poet Robert Browning's imagination led him to write a speech in the words of eleventh century Italian painter del Sarto. The artist was a technical master but his paintings lacked feeling and intensity, a handicap that del Sarto pained over. Browning wrote, "Had I been two, another and myself, yet this must be so because no one is perfect. There is always something missing… Ah, but a man's reach should exceed his grasp, or what's a heaven for?"

"Let sleeping dogs lie."
Charles Dickens (1812–1870)

Charles Dickens quoted this proverb in his novel *David Copperfield* (1849). The phrase is muttered in repentance by the clever Uriah Heep to his patron, partner and then victim, Mr. Wickfield, after being scorned by the latter. Heep asks Mr. Wickfield for a more permanent partnership with Wickfield's daughter, Agnes. Wickfield begins to break down, and to strengthen his position again, Heep comes back with, "Let sleeping dogs lie—who wants to rouse 'em? I don't." The saying hints that a bad idea is best forgotten quickly.

"Let the chips fall where they may."
Roscoe Conkling (1829–1888)

> Roscoe Conkling was a U.S. senator from New York and advisor to president Ulysses S. Grant. The famous expression originated in an address he made to the Republican national convention in June 1880, in which he rose to nominate Grant for an unprecedented third term. The complete quote is, "He will hew to the right line, let the chips fall where they may." The hotly contested convention finally nominated Ohio senator James A. Garfield on the thirty-sixth ballot. But Conkling's flattery didn't go unrewarded. Chester A. Arthur of New York, a protégé, was nominated as Garfield's running mate. He succeeded to the presidency after Garfield was assassinated in 1881.

"No man's credit is as good as his money."
Henry Van Dyke (1852–1933)

> An accomplished man of letters, Presbyterian minister Henry Van Dyke spent eighteen years as professor of literature at Princeton University and three years as U.S. ambassador to the Netherlands prior to America's entry into World War I. He penned the memorable line in his memoir, *America for Me* (1921), explaining to his cash-strapped European counterparts how trade with the U.S. could be expedited.

"What this country needs is a good five cent cigar."
Thomas Riley Marshall (1854–1929)

As Woodrow Wilson's vice president, Thomas Marshall might have remained obscure to history had he not uttered this expression during a senate debate on inflation. The quotation was made memorable by Wilson's political opponents in an attempt to embarrass the Democrats prior to mid-term elections in 1914. After leaving office in 1920, Marshall returned to his native Indiana, got rich and published a memoir.

"But is it art?"
Rudyard Kipling (1865–1936)

This trite question is frequently heard in museums and art galleries around the world, particularly when contemporary, abstract or minimalist art is on display. Capturing both the ambivalence and insecurity which artists, critics and audiences feel about the sometimes absurd works of art offered under the guise of modernism, Rudyard Kipling puts this line into the mouth of one of the keenest and most unforgiving critics, the devil himself. The line appears in stanza seven of Kipling's satirical poem, *The Conundrum of the Workshops* (1892). He speaks from the perspective of the artist laying himself bare before the critical question, "It's pretty, but is it Art?" The capital

A in Art suggests a lofty, objective analysis, indicating Kipling's philosophy that art is meant to be virtuous.

"My lips are sealed."
Stanley Baldwin (1867–1947)

Stanley Baldwin had the unfortunate task of presiding over the British government during the tumultuous short reign of Edward VIII, the dashing and popular bachelor who turned his back on the crown to marry American divorcée Wallis Warfield Simpson. The taciturn Tory leader orchestrated a consensus of silence within the British press as the dramatic events unfolded following the death of King George V on January 20, 1936. The statement signaled to the assembled journalists that they should leave; Baldwin could reveal nothing.

"No matter how thin you slice it, it's still baloney."
Alfred E. Smith (1873–1944)

Defeated by Herbert Hoover in the presidential campaign of 1928, Democrat Alfred E. Smith, four-time governor of New York, was a colorful and popular politician because he maintained his connection with the common people. In the campaign of 1936, when asked about Franklin D. Roosevelt's "New Deal," he replied, "No matter how thin you slice it, it's still baloney."

"The lunatics have taken over the asylum."

Richard Rowland (1880–1947)

> Hollywood screenwriter Richard Rowland was commentating on the formation of United Artists Corporation in 1919. To escape from the suffocating control of artless movie producers, Charles Chaplin, Mary Pickford, Douglas Fairbanks and D. W. Griffith formed their own film corporation, which originally was intended to finance and distribute quality independent films. The move was seen as insane at the time, but United Artists quickly became one of the largest production companies in Hollywood, turning out hundreds of successful, critically acclaimed films.

"Include me out."

Samuel Goldwyn (1882–1974)

> Hollywood film producer Samuel Goldwyn became famous as much for his outlandish locution as for his spectacular movies. Dozens of ridiculous quotations known as "Goldwynisms" are attributed to him. In fact, when Goldwynisms became a national curiosity, the public relations department of his studio began manufacturing such "quotations" to generate publicity. This particular gaffe, one of his most famous, is believed to have been said in regard to a proposed partnership on a movie project. On March 1, 1945, in an address at Balliol College

at Oxford, Goldwyn said, "For years I have been known for saying 'Include me out;' but today I am giving it up forever."

"Because it's there."
George Leigh Mallory (1886–1924)

Why would anyone want to climb a mountain? George Leigh Mallory was the British mountaineer who gave the world what continues to be the only answer to this perplexing question. It wasn't just any mountain he was being asked about climbing. It was the big one: Mount Everest in the Himalayas. Ironically, less than a year later, Mallory became one of the many climbers who died attempting to scale the world's tallest peak. The summit would not be reached for the first time until another generation had passed, and Sir Edmund Hillary and Tenzing Norgay ascended to the top of the world on May 29, 1953.

"Win this one for the Gipper."
Knute Rockne (1888–1931)

Knute Rockne achieved fame as the head football coach for the University of Notre Dame (Indiana), where he posted 105 victories against only 12 defeats. He was known for his fiery locker-room pep talks, including his memorable "Gipper" speech in 1928. Rockne told his players that former Notre Dame star player George

Gipp, on his deathbed, had asked the coach to win a game in his honor. "This is that game," Rockne told his players, and an inspired Notre Dame team defeated heavily favored Army. Recounted in the melodramatic movie Knute Rockne, All American (1940), starring Ronald Reagan as Gipp, the main facts of the story are true. Actually, the opportunistic Rockne had already used "the Gipper" to good effect on a number of occasions before the dramatic victory of 1928. During the presidential campaign of 1980, the phrase was frequently repeated in support of Ronald Reagan's candidacy.

"The last of the red hot mamas."
Jack Yellen (1892–1991)

The famous phrase belonged to Sophie Tucker, a flamboyant vaudeville star and cabaret singer of the 1920s and 1930s, who was known for her lusty and throaty rendition of *Some of These Days*. Her song, *I'm the Last of the Red Hot Mommas*, written by American tunesmith Jack Yellen in 1928, so perfectly suited Tucker that it became a permanent part of her showcase. Yellen wrote many other memorable songs, including *Ain't She Sweet?* and *Happy Days are Here Again*, the campaign song of the Democratic party in 1932.

"Believe it or not."
Robert L. Ripley (1893–1949)

Robert Ripley was a sports illustrator for the New York Globe. Plagued with a case of artist's block one afternoon in 1918, he searched through his notes and realized they contained news of several sporting oddities. He quickly created an illustrated feature called *Champs & Chumps* about a man who jumped backwards and an undefeated female wrestler. He showed it to one of his colleagues who concluded his review by saying, "I guess you can believe it or not." Ripley seized upon the phrase and, before handing it in, changed the title to Believe It or Not. It was an instant success and readers clamored for more. Ripley's career as a chronicler of strange and unlikely phenomena, bizarre coincidences and freaks of nature from around the world was launched. He quickly garnered a reputation for flamboyance and extravagance and was voted the most popular person in America in 1923. Believe It or Not was syndicated in hundreds of newspapersworldwide, and published in dozens of paperback collections. The idea was also the basis for a radio series, a television series, and a chain of museums dedicated to the bizarre.

"Candy is dandy but liquor is quicker."
Ogden Nash (1902–1971)

Ogden Nash's catch phrase was the entire text of his poem, *Reflections on Ice-Breaking.* An American original, Nash used humorous puns in verse form with his gift of lyric and biting satire, while working at Doubleday, Page & Co. and The New Yorker. His oft-quoted ditty explains the best technique for creating a climate conducive to introducing a man and a woman.

"Back to the drawing boards!"
Curtis Arnoux Peters (1904–1968)

Used today by some to mean nothing more than "time to go back to work," this popular phrase can be traced back to a celebrated World War II era New Yorker cartoon by the sophisticated artist Peter Arno (Curtis Arnoux Peters). The cartoon depicts an air flight proving ground as a plane crashes in front of a dismayed group of military officers. The designer, hands clutched together and rolled-up plans under his arm, turns from the scene with a supercilious smile. The caption reads, "Well, back to the old drawing board."

"Nice guys finish last."
Leo Durocher (1905–1991)

Leo Durocher was born on his kitchen table—an occurrence that, if anything, builds character. He was a rookie with the 1927 Yankees, the team of Lou Gehrig and Babe Ruth, and later became manager of the Brooklyn Dodgers and the New York Giants, chalking up more years in baseball than almost anybody. So what does he have to complain about? Well, nothing. "Nice guys finish last" was a comment Durocher made about the New York Giants while he was managing the Dodgers because, although the Giants were nice guys, Durocher was convinced they would finish last.

"He cried all the way to the bank."
Wladziu Valentino Liberace (1919–1987)

The flamboyant showman Liberace made a fortune in the 1960s as a classical pianist, although critics insisted his success had nothing to do with serious music and furthermore that his appeal was based on cheap sentimentalism. Such criticism, however, did nothing to impair the popularity of his television programs, recordings, books and personal appearances. Liberace's self-effacing but highly visible handler was his brother, George. On one occasion, when the entertainer was asked if he was not hurt by what a critic had said, his studied reply was, "Well, I know it hurt George. This morning, poor George cried all the way to the bank."

CHAPTER 6
WHO REPEATED THAT?

Recycled Quotations in New Contexts

"Don't look a gift horse in the mouth."
François Rabelais (1495–1553)

The famous phrase is taken from French humorist François Rabelais' *Gargantua and Pantagruel* (1532–1564), Book I, chapter two. A proverbial expression of superstition, Rabelais used it to describe the giant Gargantua's precocious and gullible character: "He always looks a gift horse in the mouth." This mock heroic chronicle was first published in parts beginning in 1532. The phrase later appeared in *The Proverbs of John Heywood* (1546) and Cervantes' Don Quixote (1615) and came to mean "don't be ungrateful."

"Eat, drink and be merry."
Thomas Jordan (c.1612–1685)

English poet Thomas Jordan's song, The Epicure, personifies the carefree lifestyle. The song is from a banquet scene in Jordan's poem Triumphs of London, which was performed as a pageant as early as 1675. The phrase, sometimes attributed to Shakespeare and merely recycled by Jordan, was originally found in both the old and new testaments of the Bible. Ecclesiastes, chapter 8, verse 15, reads, "A man hath no better thing under the sun than to eat, and to drink, and to be merry." And Luke, chapter 12, verse 19, contains, "Soul, thou hast much goods laid up for many years; take thine ease, eat, drink, and be merry."

"Facts are stubborn things."
John Adams (1735–1826)

Long before his election to the presidency in 1796, John Adams was a Harvard-educated trial attorney from Boston. Despite his strong colonial sentiments, he agreed to defend five British soldiers accused of dereliction of duty during the infamous Boston Massacre in 1770. "Facts are stubborn things," he said in his closing argument, "and whatever may be our wishes, our inclinations or the dictates of our passions, they cannot alter the state of facts and evidence." Prior to this usage, the phrase appeared in Book X, Chapter 1 of French satirist Alain Rene Lesage's magnum opus Gil Blas (1735), which was widely acclaimed in England and the American colonies. One can only speculate whether the well-read Adams converted the phrase with the hope of making it his own.

"What hath God wrought!"
Samuel F. B. Morse (1791–1872)

This quote is often attributed to American inventor Samuel Morse, who transmitted these words as the first message sent by telegraph on May 24, 1844. The quote, however, may be found in the fourth book of the Old Testament, Numbers, chapter 23, verse 23, which describes the people of Israel bolstered by the Lord. The complete verse says, "Surely no enchantment against Jacob, neither any divination against Israel: according to this time it shall be said of Jacob and of Israel, What hath God wrought!" Morse's seminal telegraph message was sent from Baltimore to Washington, D.C., a distance of about forty-five miles.

"Time flies."
Edward Fitzgerald (1809–1883)

English poet Edward Fitzgerald, translator of *The Rubaiyat of Omar Khayyám*, freely adapted the work of this twelfth-century Persian poet. While Fitzgerald didn't precisely write "time flies," the essence of the following lines has been so interpreted.

Come fill the cup, and in the Fire of Spring
The Winter Garment of Repentance fling:
The bird of time has but a little way
To fly—and lo! the bird is on the wing.

However, the saying may be traced as far back as Roman poet Virgil (70–19 BCE), who included the Latin proverb Tempus fugit, "time flies," in his collection of didactic poems entitled Georgics.

"Never complain and never explain."
Henry Ford (1863–1947)

The phrase is usually associated with American industrialist Henry Ford, commonly derided for his innovative ideas, who found it a convenient device to dismiss his erstwhile critics. Ford, however, merely popularized the saying on the American side of the Atlantic. It originated with British statesman Benjamin Disraeli (1804–1881), prime minister of England. Disraeli, popular novelist and consummate diplomat, returned from negotiations with Russia and Turkey declaring he had "brought back peace with honour." British author John Morley's biography Life of Gladstone (1903) is the source of the quotation, which Disraeli uttered to his implacable political enemy, prime minister William Gladstone.

"There's no use crying over spilt milk."
H. G. Wells (1866–1946)

When English novelist H. G. Wells wrote, "It's no good crying over spilt milk," in *You Can't Be Too Careful* (1942), he was recycling an old proverb that had previously appeared as "It's no use to cry over what's done and can't be helped," in *A Connecticut Yankee in King Arthur's Court* (1889) by American humorist Mark Twain. Neither author deserves the credit for this saying, however, because English printer William Caxton (c.1422–1491) published the first known version in 1484 in Aesope. His original admonishment, "The thyrd [doctrine] is that thow take no sorrowe of the thynge lost whiche may not be recovered," has evolved and re-appeared in print many times.

"Why don't you come up and see me sometime?"
Mae West (1892–1980)

Nearly everyone associates this classic line of flirtation with actress and writer Mae West and the film *She Done Him Wrong* (1933), in which she entices Cary Grant with the question, "Why don't you come up sometime and see me?" Miss West had brought the line along from her successful Broadway show *Diamond Lil* (1928). But it was not until 1939 and the film My Little Chickadee that moviegoers heard West, with transparent self parody, put the question to comedian W. C. Fields in its now popular intonation, "Why don't you come up and see me sometime?"

"We was robbed!"
Joe Jacobs (1896–1940)

> Joe Jacobs, a promoter and manager of prize fighters in the 1930s, handled the stateside bouts for the German heavyweight champion Max Schmeling. Schmeling was defeated by American fighter Jack Sharkey in 1932, and immediately after the fight, Joe Jacobs snatched hold of the radio microphone and shouted to millions of listeners, "We was robbed!" Jacobs may or may not have remembered a similar incident five years before, when in 1927, pugilist Jack Dempsey was defeated by Gene Tunny after a notorious "long count" in the championship bout. Tunny was barely able to avoid the ten count, but then rallied to defeat Dempsey, who later told reporters, "I have been robbed of my championship."

"Low man on the totem pole."
H. Allen Smith (1907–1976)

> A totem pole is a carved wooden post, often of great size, on which symbolic carvings represent the distinctive ancestry and spirituality of a given Native American clan. The symbols are arranged hierarchically, with the most important at the top. Fred Allen (1894–1956), a popular radio comedian before the days of television, was asked to write an introduction to a collection of humorous writings by his friend H. Allen Smith. There, the sardonic Allen quipped, "If Smith were an Indian, he

would be the low man on any totem pole." Smith was so taken with Allen's remark that he entitled his next book Low Man on the Totem Pole (1941).

"We have met they enemy and they is us."
Walt Kelly (1913–1973)

Cartoonist Walt Kelly, creator of the long running and frequently allegorical comic strip Pogo, was commissioned by the U.S. Park Service to create an anti-littering poster in 1970. Featuring Pogo in a forest setting surrounded by garbage, presumably not far from his Okefenokee Swamp home, the poster's message struck a national nerve and quickly became a part of our lexicon of popular phraseology. What is not widely known is that Kelly lifted the phrase from a dispatch by naval captain Oliver Hazard Perry (1785–1819) in a skirmish with the British on Lake Erie during the War of 1812. What Perry reported to his superiors the following day was, "We have met the enemy and they are ours."

"The chickens have come home to roost."
Malcolm X (1925–1965)

The poem, *The Curse of Kehama* (1810), by British poet laureate Robert Southey (1774–1843), begins with the motto, "Curses are like young chickens; they always come home to roost." The implication is that our misfortunes are the result of our own previous ill-considered actions. The phrase can still be used with considerable effect. Malcolm X, leader of the Organization of Afro-American Unity, created a furor when he said the assassination of president John F. Kennedy was a case of "chickens coming home to roost." To quiet the resulting uproar, Elija Muhammad, leader of the rival Nation of Islam, immediately repudiated the statement.

"A chicken in every pot."
Republican Party campaign slogan (1932)

King Henry IV of France (1553–1610) is most remembered for granting universal religious freedom in his *Edict of Nantes* (1598). At his coronation in 1589, Henry vowed to work for French prosperity and was quoted as saying that he looked forward to the time when "every peasant will have a chicken in his pot on Sunday." Centuries later, the Republican Party adopted the quote as a political slogan and campaign promise for the presidential election of 1932. Unfortunately, "a chicken in every pot" only served to remind voters of the harsh realities of the Great Depression, and Republican incumbent Herbert Hoover lost the election to New York's governor, Democrat Franklin D. Roosevelt.

About the Author

Joseph S. Ajlouny was born in Detroit in 1958, the only son of immigrants from Ramallah, Palestine. His father was a member of the US Army who served in Japan and South Korea during the Korean War. After raising six children, his mother became a public-school ESL educator. Both were active members of their church and community organizations. Joseph graduated from Wayne State University in Detroit in 1979 with a B.A. in Journalism. A London, England, based art gallery and print publisher hired him as a writer and promoter of fine art, including original limited-edition prints, rare books, and manuscripts. He attended night classes at Detroit College of Law (now Michigan State University College of Law) and earned a J.D. in 1983, but never fully engaged in the practice of law, preferring to make a career in art and literature instead. A series of opportunities took him from the newspaper syndication business to book publishing and a thriving literary and talent agency. In 1998 he incorporated these various concerns into an umbrella organization called the Federal Bureau of Entertainment. The principal focus of FBE was the development, production, and staging of one-person stage shows featuring notable British actors whose performances highlighted important literary texts from Shakespeare to Orwell. Now in ungainly but blissful retirement, Joseph has resumed his writing career and is devoting himself to touring theatre projects and topical research in Great Lakes history. He is a Reader in History at the Library of Congress and the William Clements Library at the University of Michigan.

Index

A

Absence makes the heart grow fonder 15
All I know is what I read in the papers 44
All is fair in love and war 53
All that glitters is not gold 30
And I don't mean maybe 68
Ask me no questions, and I'll tell you no lies 73

B

Back to the drawing boards! 89
Bad news travels fast 3
Beauty is in the eye of the beholder 42
Because it's there 86
Beggars can't be choosers 5
Believe it or not 88
Best laid plans of mice and men often go astray, The 50
Bird in the hand is worth two in the bush, A 31
Blood is thicker than water 38
Born with a silver spoon in his mouth 29
Buck stops here, The 44
Build a better mousetrap and the world will beat a path to your door 43
But is it art 83

C

Candy is dandy but liquor is quicker 89
Charity begins at home 32
Chicken in every pot, A 98
Chickens have come home to roost, The 97
Chip off the old block, A 12
Cleanliness is next to godliness 33

D

Damn the torpedoes, full speed ahead 65
Devil can cite scripture for his purpose, The 7
Do as I say, not as I do 8
Don't look a gift horse in the mouth 91
Don't shoot till you see the whites of their eyes 35

E

Eat, drink and be merry 91

End justifies the means, The 10
Every man for himself 4

F

Face that launched a thousand ships, The 71
Facts are stubborn things 92
First in war, first in peace, and first in the hearts of his countrymen 13
First we kill all the lawyers. 62
Fools rush in where angels fear to tread 28
Forewarned is forearmed 6
Friend in need is a friend indeed, A 2
Full of the milk of human kindness 60

G

Genius is one percent inspiration and ninety-nine percent perspiration 21
Give him enough rope and he will hang himself 54
Go west, young man 42
God helps those who help themselves 27
Good fences make good neighbors 67

H

He cried all the way to the bank 90
He had the Midas touch 63
he mighty Casey has struck out 23
He was as sober as a judge 12
Hell hath no fury like a woman scorned 64
here's no use crying over spilt milk 94
Hope springs eternal 11

I

I can resist everything but temptation 22
I don't believe in God because I don't believe in Mother Goose 22
I have it here in black and white 8
I hear you loud and clear 66
I must go down to the sea again 55
I regret that I have but one life to give my country 50
I'll turn over a new leaf 30
I'm all ears. 71
If a man bites a dog, that's news 20
If you can't stand the heat, get out of the kitchen 45
In one fell swoop 61
Include me out 85
It made his mouth water 9
It makes no sense to flog a dead horse 2
It seemed so near and yet so far away 17
It was a dark and stormy night 16

It was six of one and half a dozen of the other..78
It's better to die fighting than to live in slavery.....................................23
It's like playing tennis without a net...54
It's not what it's cracked up to be..13

K

Knowledge is power...70

L

Last of the red hot mamas, Thei..87
Laugh and the world laughs with you; weep, and you weep alone............21
Leave no stone unturned...1
Let sleeping dogs lie...81
Let the chips fall where they may...82
Let the punishment fit the crime...66
Let them eat cake...36
Little learning is a dangerous thing, A..65
Look before you leap..28
Love conquers all..3
Low man on the totem pole...96
Lunatics have taken over the asylum, The..85

M

Man's home is his castle, A..6
Man's reach should exceed his grasp or what's a heaven for, A...............81
Mary had a little lamb..14
Master of all he surveys...49
Men seldom make passes at girls who wear glasses..................................24
Might makes right..59
Music hath charms to soothe the savage beast...47
My lips are sealed...84

N

Necessity is the mother of invention...1
Never complain and never explain...94
Nice guys finish last...89
No man's credit is as good as his money...82
No matter how thin you slice it, it's still balone.......................................84
No sooner said than done...27
No time like the present...72
Not much worse for wear...74
Nothing is certain but death and taxes..48
Nothing is easy for a dying man..48
Now is the time for all good men to come to the aid of their party.........20

O

O Romeo, Romeo! wherefore art thou Romeo 62
One good turn deserves another 69
Out of sight is out of mind 75

P

Penny saved is a penny earned, A...34
People who live in glass houses shouldn't throw stones 32
Peter Piper picked a peck of pickled peppers...76
Play it again, Sam 56
Plot thickens, The...10
Public be damned, The..19
Put your best foot forward 18

R

Remember the Alamo...16
Rose is a rose is a rose 55

S

Sharp tongue grows sharper with constant use, A 51
Shot heard round the world, The 79
Should auld acquaintance be forgot, and days of auld lang syne 37
Sound mind in a sound body, A 4
Spare the rod and spoil the child 59
Stone walls do not a prison make 9
Survival of the fittest..38

T

Take care of the minutes, for the hours will take care of themselves 72
That government is best which governs least...35
That's another story 73
That's chicken feed..77
That's one small step for man, one giant leap for mankind..56
The best is yet to come..53
There but for the grace of God go I 47
There shall be no love lost..63
There's a sucker born every minute 40
There's an exception to every rule...52
There's no getting blood out of a turnip 78
They have a skeleton in their closet 19
This is adding insult to injuries..34
This is war...79
Time flies...93
Tis better to have loved and lost than never to have loved at all...................................40
To the victor belongs the spoils..14

v

W

Watched pot never boils, A 41
We have met they enemy and they is us 97
We was robbed 96
What has posterity done for us 74
What hath God wrought 93
What this country needs is a good five cent cigar 83
When in Rome, do as the Romans do 64
Where there's a will, there's a way 8
Why don't you come up and see me sometime 95
Win this one for the Gipper 86
With malice toward none and charity for all 80
Woman of a certain age, A 51

Y

You can fool all the people some of the time and some of the people all the time,
    but you can not fool all the people all the time 39
You can lead a horse to water but you can't make him drink 5
You drive for show but putt for dough 25
You have hit the nail on the head 69
You'll be damned if you do and damned if you don't 77

The Fresh Ink Group

Publishing
Free Memberships
Share & Read Free Stories, Essays, Articles
Free-Story Newsletter
Writing Contests

❧

Books
E-books
Amazon Bookstore

❧

Authors
Editors
Artists
Professionals
Publishing Services
Publisher Resources

❧

Members' Websites
Members' Blogs
Social Media

FreshInkGroup.com

Email: info@FreshInkGroup.com

Twitter: @FreshInkGroup

Google+: Fresh Ink Group

Facebook.com/FreshInkGroup

LinkedIn: Fresh Ink Group

About.me/FreshInkGroup

Fresh Ink Group

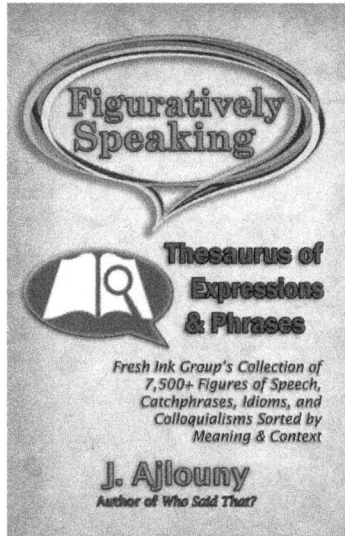

Figuratively Speaking
Thesaurus of Expressions & Phrases

By J. Ajlouny

A figure of speech is an expression in which the words are used, but not in their literal sense, to create a more forceful or dramatic meaning. They are often in the form of metaphors, similes, and hyperbole. "A fountain of knowledge" is a good example. "Stretching the truth" is another.

With *Figurative Speaking,* we finally have a thesaurus to discover these phrases' origins and the sources of their meanings. Categories include:

- Attitudes
- Body Types
- Competition
- Creature Comforts
- Letting Loose
- Ethics
- Influence
- Life, Health, & Death
- Money
- Personal Space
- Personality Types
- Speech
- Thinking Power
- Time
- Trouble, Turmoil, & Commotion
- The World of Work

Whether reading it for fun, researching phrases you use, or studying the symbolic foundations of our language, *Figuratively Speaking* is the resource you'll reach for time and again.

FreshInkGroup.com

www.ingramcontent.com/pod-product-compliance
Lightning Source LLC
Chambersburg PA
CBHW051637050426

42443CB00025B/413